Silent Marauders

Also by Graeme Cook

Wings of Glory
None but the Valiant
Commandos in Action
Spotlight on Aircraft
Air Adventures
Break Out!
Sea Adventures
Weird and Wonderful Ships
Weird and Wonderful Aircraft
Sea Raiders
Survival Against All Odds
Amazing Vehicles at Work

Silent Marauders

Graeme Cook

Hart-Davis, MacGibbon London

Granada Publishing Limited
First published in Great Britain 1976 by Hart-Davis, MacGibbon Ltd.
Frogmore, St Albans Hertfordshire AL2 2NF and
3 Upper James Street London W1R 4BP

Copyright © 1976 by Graeme Cook

ISBN 0 246 10784 7

Printed in Great Britain by
Northumberland Press Limited
Gateshead
Richard Clay (The Chaucer Press) Ltd,
Bungay, Suffolk

Contents

		page
	Introduction	7
1	British Submarines in the First World War	11
2	British Submarines in the Second World War	62
3	Midget Submarines	124
	Conclusion	153
	Bibliography	157

To
Elma and Nick

Introduction

The element of surprise is perhaps the most potent weapon in the armoury of an aggressor. With the advantage of surprise on his side, numerical strength is often of secondary importance. The ability to remain unseen before, during and after the launching of an attack has, since man first bore weapons of war, posed the cardinal problem for the tactician.

For those who fought on land in past wars, the difficulty of achieving this end was partially overcome by the use of camouflage, but for the world's navies the problem was infinitely more difficult. A warship capable of delivering an effective attack, no matter how well disguised, invariably stuck out like a sore thumb at sea. Only in adverse weather conditions had the attacker any chance of remaining unseen, but then he was faced with the very problem of delivering an attack under such conditions. Also, the mantle of darkness was no safe cover for an attacker for he was then faced with the problem of navigating on to his target.

Ever since men first waged war at sea, sailors have puzzled over how this elusive element of surprise could be gained. After countless attempts at camouflaging their warships, it became clear that there could be only one sure way of succeeding in their efforts to achieve 'invisibility' and that was to devise a method of travelling *beneath* the surface of the water, using the very sea itself as a cloak under which to hide.

Inventors over the centuries racked their brains to produce a submersible vessel capable of underwater travel even for short periods. But without satisfactory building materials or the manufacturing capability their efforts were thwarted at every turn. In the very early experiments submarine-builders had not the metals capable of withstanding the tremendous pressures exerted upon a hull underwater nor had they the means by which to propel such a vessel. Furthermore, medical science had not advanced to a stage where the problems of remaining alive below water were understood. In these very early experiments, an undersea voyage invariably resulted in the suffocating demise of the submariner and without the technical or medical skill to carry out a searching post-mortem, there was rarely any clear evidence as to why he had failed.

The United States can justly claim the title 'mother of the submarine' for it was in that country that the first serious attempts at building and using a working submersible were made. It fell to a young American student, David Bushnell, to provide his country with her first 'submarine'.

Around the time of the American War of Independence Bushnell discovered a means by which gunpowder could be exploded under water. He reasoned that, given a suitable craft to transport him *unseen* to a target, he could inflict serious damage or even sink an enemy warship by penetrating its harbour and setting his explosive to blow up beneath the warship's waterline. Having successfully developed a bomb with which to destroy his target he was posed with the problem of actually getting it there. Necessity being the mother of invention, he built the *Turtle*, completed in 1776.

Bushnell's *Turtle* was aptly named, for it resembled two turtle shells clamped together to form an egg-shape. Built of wood, it carried a one-man crew. The crewman had to be both extremely courageous and extraordinarily dextrous for he had to perform the navigation, guidance and attack single-handed.

The craft was without an engine and propelled both up and down and in the horizontal plane by hand. Close by the watertight hatch at the top of *Turtle* was a screw-shaped device which the submariner wound in an anti-clockwise direction to submerge. There was yet another 'screw' at the front of the boat which the operator wound to propel the boat along. The bottom of the boat consisted of a water tank which, when the boat was required to dive, was flooded by the use of a foot-operated valve. When it was required to surface the submariner had to pump out the water with a hand pump. A small conning tower on top of the *Turtle* was fitted with glass windows which allowed the crewman limited forward vision. A hand-operated rudder attached to the rear of the boat gave directional guidance. Bushnell's explosive 'bomb' was attached to the rear of the boat and operated by a clockwork mechanism. The intention was that it should be attached to the target ship's hull by means of a spike driven into the wooden belly of the ship.

When Bushnell had tested and prepared his submarine for action, a target was chosen. The British warship *Eagle* was selected for this first-ever submarine attack. At the time, she was anchored in New York Harbour along with other ships of the fleet.

Bushnell was a man of considerable intelligence and although he had immense faith in his invention, he had no intention of being the 'guinea pig' who would undertake the attack. Sergeant Ezra Lee was the man upon whom this signal honour was to be bestowed and, on the appointed night, he set off into New York Harbour. He succeeded in reaching *Eagle* and positioning himself under the ship's hull but then he discovered a serious flaw in the whole operation. Bushnell had not taken into account that the bottom of the British warship had a coating of copper. Lee found it impossible to penetrate the copper with the bomb-spike and after some struggle was forced to abandon the venture.

When he eventually surfaced, the first rays of dawn were spreading over the water and his craft was spotted and chased by British sailors. His speed was seriously impaired by the weight of the bomb so he discarded it and, turning his forward screw with all his strength, made off. The pursuing British sailors, wary of the orb that bobbed in the water, gave it a wide berth. It is as well that they did because half an hour later it exploded.

Although Bushnell's submarine had failed to sink *Eagle*, the raid was a partial success for, as a result of it, the British fleet put out of harbour at full speed.

This and the raids that followed had an almost comic ring to them, certainly for those of us today who marvel at the evolution of underwater craft and compare the devastating power of today's nuclear submarines with early attempts at using a submersible vessel as a weapon of war. However, had it not been for these first attempts it is unlikely that there would be a nuclear submarine force today, and perhaps the whole course of world history might have been altered.

Britain, once the most powerful maritime nation in the world, has probably suffered more than any other country as a

result of submarine attack. Twice within the space of thirty
years she was brought within a hair's breadth of defeat because
of German submarine warfare, notably in the Atlantic. It
is therefore not surprising that the Royal Navy has built up
over the years one of the most potent submarine fleets in the
world, an ever-vigilant peace-keeping force. In two world wars,
the Royal Navy Submarine Service has produced some of the
world's finest submariners who have built up an outstanding
tradition of courage and determination. This book is about the
men of that Service and their deeds which remain today an inspiration to those who man our nuclear submarines.

1

British Submarines in The First World War

At the outbreak of the First World War, the Royal Navy had some seventy-four submarines of various classes in full commission, dispersed at bases in Britain and throughout the world. Sixty-five of these boats were to be found in Britain itself, divided up among nine flotillas stationed at ports on the east and south coasts. The largest flotilla, the Eighth, under the command of Commodore Roger Keyes, was based at Harwich and operated from the depot ships *Adamant* and *Maidstone*. Known as the Overseas Flotilla, it comprised eight D- and nine E-class submarines. The remaining flotillas were based at Dover, Chatham, Humber, Tyne and Forth with the task of operating along the east coast and in the Straits of Dover. Within hours of the alert that Britain was at war, British submarines were heading out to sea.

The role determined for the British submarine in the First World War differed substantially from that of its German counterpart. The U-boat's primary functions were to strangle Britain into defeat by attacking her merchantmen and in addition equalize, or at least lessen, Britain's surface naval strength by sinking her warships. The British Admiralty, on the other hand, reserved a curious attitude towards its submarine force. Since the submarine had never been tried in battle and therefore there was no yardstick by which to judge its proper role in war, it was regarded as something of an oddity and because of its 'underhanded' mode of attack, a singularly un-British weapon. Their Lordships thought it not quite 'fair play' to use the submarine in sneak attacks. Naval tradition had insisted upon the warring fleets coming face to face in battle and slogging it out.

The result of this somewhat naïve attitude was the relegation of the submarine to the role of forward scout; a sort of reconnaissance vessel which would penetrate enemy waters and keep watch on enemy fleet movements with a view to warning the British Fleet if the Germans seemed to be preparing for a sortie. Indeed, submarine commanders were given instructions that their job as spies was all important and took preference over the sinking of enemy ships. This attitude was to be brought to a very abrupt halt when, only days after the opening of hostilities the German U-21 sank the British light cruiser *Pathfinder*. From that moment on, it was 'gloves off' with British submarine commanders. The submarine, even in those early hours of the war, had clearly shown that it had teeth and could bite.

Submarines of the Overseas Flotilla took up patrol lines off the Germans' main fleet base at Wilhelmshaven, patrolling the waters of the Heligoland Bight and lying in wait for the German Fleet to emerge. It was in these waters that a young lieutenant commander by the name of Max Horton was to win his spurs and begin a career destined to culminate years later in his being hailed as one of the greatest of Britain's submarine commanders.

The war was only days old when the British cruiser *Pathfinder* fell to the torpedoes of the German submarine U-21. Horton evened the score a week later while patrolling in the Heligoland Bight in the E-class boat E-9. His submarine, having lain on the sea-bed all night, rose to periscope depth at dawn and its commander scanned the sea with his periscope. The periscope's eye had traced only a few degrees when Horton halted its progress and fixed on a shape on the horizon. Steaming towards his position was the German light cruiser *Hela*, although at this point Horton knew only that she was a German warship, her identity was to be proved later.

The *Hela* was a mere two miles off when Horton first caught sight of her so there was little time for attack preparations. Horton's preliminary orders brought the crew to action. For the first time a British submarine was going into action in earnest and the success of the action rested squarely upon Horton's shoulders and his good judgement. He was aided by a somewhat crude computing device, known as the 'Is–Was', which gave the deflection angle on which torpedoes were fired, based on enemy speed, enemy inclination and torpedo setting speed. It was automatic and fitted to a gyro-compass repeater. Although rather primitive, it did take a fair amount of the guess-work out of attack situations.

With the bow-caps open on the forward torpedo tubes, allowing them to be flooded ready for firing, and the first lieutenant poised to shoot on the order from Horton, he brought the submarine round into attack position. The *Hela* stayed on a steady course ploughing through the water, unaware of the danger that awaited her then when she had come within 600 yards of E-9, two torpedoes shot away from the submarine amid a flurry of bubbles. Immediately Horton ordered 'Down periscope' and the first lieutenant took the boat into the depths. The seconds ticked by and the crew waited expectantly for the tell-tale thuds and explosions that would signal hits. The wait was agonizingly long but at last the pronounced sound of two explosions telegraphed the message that both torpedoes had found the target.

E-9 was by then manoeuvring to a new position, away from the trail of bubbles left by her torpedoes which would give away her position and bring guns to bear on her. After what Horton considered to be a safe period of time he brought E-9 to periscope depth and fixed the periscope on the *Hela*, which he found to be listing badly and on the point of sinking; but she was not yet done for and gunners opened up at the submarine, forcing Horton to seek succour in the depths. He took E-9 deep, out of harm's way, secure in the knowledge that there was (at that time) neither a sonic method of detecting a submarine's presence nor of attacking her beneath the waves.

Horton lay deep for almost an hour before he ventured another look at his handiwork. All that remained of the German cruiser were bits of floating wreckage strewn over the surface of the water. Already, however, German destroyers were scouring the area for E-9 and Horton, having confirmed his success, prudently retreated from the scene.

The following month Horton, again on patrol in the Bight, sent the German destroyer S.116 to the bottom, a signal achievement since a fast-running destroyer was no mean target to hit. His ability to score such a victory was a prelude to the success he was to enjoy later in other waters.

The Baltic

It became clear to the Admiralty that the German Naval High Command was to rely upon her submarine strength to alter the balance of power at sea and that she had no intention of risking her High Seas Fleet in a face-to-face encounter with the British Grand Fleet. For the time being at least, the Germans were to keep their capital ships secure in the safe waters of the Bight where no British warships would venture in strength. Furthermore the Germans used the Baltic for fleet exercises and, since it was superior in strength to the Russian Fleet, it had little to fear from that quarter. German warships were making to the Baltic via the Kiel canal with impunity and carrying out exercises there without fear of attack.

The Admiralty resolved to hinder these exercises and prove that no waters were safe for the German Fleet; and there was but one way of doing this: by sending a submarine force into the Baltic by way of the Kattegat and through the narrow and shallow Sound, the stretch of water between Denmark and Sweden. The passage itself into the Baltic was to be no trifling matter, since at one point in the Sound the water was so shallow that a submarine could not dive. This meant penetrating the Sound by night.

Three E-class submarines were chosen for the mission into the Baltic: E-1 (Lieutenant Commander Noel Laurence), E-9 (Lieutenant Commander Max Horton) and E-11 (Lieutenant Commander Martin Dunbar-Nasmith). Under Laurence's overall command, they were to negotiate the Sound and attack the German ships in the Baltic. The success of the operation depended upon their ability to get into the Baltic unseen. Apart from the navigational difficulties there was a further consideration for it was known that German agents both in Denmark and Sweden kept watch on the Sound, waiting for just such an attempt to slip through.

One overriding prerequisite was required of the commanders if and when they reached the Baltic. To maintain the element of surprise and ensure that the Sound was not blocked to them afterwards, they were each to wait in the Baltic until all three had arrived before launching their attacks, otherwise, if one of them immediately began attacking, the Germans would merely seal the entry to the Baltic and deny the others the chance of getting in on the fight.

15 October 1914 was the planned date for the submarines' departure from their base in Britain but E-11 suffered engine trouble and although she subsequently got under way and reached the entry to the Sound, her mechanical problems be-

came so acute that Nasmith had to abort the mission and return to base; the only action he could take under the circumstances. (As will be seen later, Nasmith was to win fame in warmer waters when E-11 was sent to the Mediterranean.)

Horton in E-9 was also dogged by mechanical troubles and lagged behind Laurence who made good headway and succeeded in reaching the Sound and the most difficult part of the journey. Laurence's E-1 slipped through the shallows and the narrow channel with her conning tower showing for all to see but she was not spotted and at last dived out of sight in the Baltic.

E-9 lagged a good five hours behind E-1 and arrived at the mouth of the Sound in daylight. Horton had to lie doggo throughout the day to await nightfall before making his attempt. This made him a whole day late, behind Laurence.

Laurence, unaware of the delay suffered by Horton and the abandonment of Nasmith's mission, found it impossible to resist the temptation of launching an attack when a German cruiser hove into sight. She was the old *Victoria Louise.* For a whole hour, Laurence stalked her until he manoeuvred the submarine into a position only 500 yards off her beam; then he fired two torpedoes. With his eyes glued to the periscope he watched their trails race towards the cruiser, one behind the other; but then to his frustration he saw the first torpedo leap out of the water then dive below the cruiser. By then the second 'fish' had been spotted and the cruiser swung head on to it, allowing the torpedo to pass harmlessly by.

Now the *Victoria Louise* was bearing down on the submarine, intent on ramming her; Laurence had to dive fast and deep out of its way, and he only just avoided being sliced in half by the cruiser's bows; when, some time later, he brought E-1 to periscope depth for a look around, he found the area infested with searching ships. His impatience had brought the hunters out and, worse still, alerted the Germans to the fact that a submarine was in the Baltic. As a result of this, they strengthened their patrols at either end of the Sound to stop any more British submarines entering, a factor which was to make Horton's passage through it all the more difficult.

Laurence, realizing that further attacks were hopeless, set course for the Latvian port of Libau which, as part of the plan of operation, was to be their base in the Baltic.

The following night Horton brought E-9 up from the depths

and nosed into the Sound. The waters of the Sound were like a mill-pond, flat and calm, undisturbed by wind. The first part of the journey through it passed without event but then Horton reached the narrow, shallow channel near Malmö. Gingerly he edged the boat forward, proceeding on one motor closed down to slow ahead. In front of him he could see the thin pencils of light emanating from searchlights in the distance and illuminating the channel. At its shallowest point, the water of the Flint Channel, as it is known, was a mere fourteen feet deep; insufficient for a submarine to dive.

Horton brought E-9 along with only her conning tower showing above the water. Absolute silence was observed in the boat and Horton, on the bridge, kept watch. Orders were given in muted whispers as the boat slid forward. Then he saw it; a destroyer little more than a hundred yards off. The submarine was bound to be spotted and Horton gave the order to dive and scrambled down the hatch out of the conning tower. But as the boat slipped deeper, she was suddenly jarred as the bottom ground on the sea-bed.

Horton stopped his motors and E-9 lay motionless upon the sea-bed, with all six feet of her periscope standards showing above the water. Surely, he thought, they must be spotted and rammed by the destroyer. The atmosphere on the boat was electric as the crew waited for the rending crash when the destroyer would slice her open ... but it did not come. Horton brought the boat up just enough to allow him to creep into the conning tower and take a look at what was happening. To his horror he saw that the destroyer was sitting only seventy yards from where he lay with motors stopped.

Horton knew he could not remain where he was. Every minute that passed brought closer the possibility of discovery. He would have to press on in the hope that his luck would hold. Running on her electric motors, E-9, with only part of her tower showing, slid forward and miraculously managed to reach deeper water without being seen. Horton took his submarine down to the sea-bed out of the destroyer's reach and remained there until dawn. He had reached the Baltic but it had been a close thing – just how close, he was to discover when he brought the boat to periscope depth and saw that he was surrounded by destroyers.

Horton took E-9 deep again and slipped away from the danger area. The air in the boat which had been submerged for so long was fast becoming foul. The atmosphere was stale and quickly brought on severe sickness among the crew. Whatever happened, Horton had to get some fresh air into the boat before his crew began collapsing at their stations. Furthermore, E-9's batteries had not been recharged for some time and were running low. At all costs he had to get on the surface and recharge them soon.

At noon he ventured a look through the periscope and saw no ships in the immediate vicinity, so he risked coming to the surface. No sooner had he done so than he saw a German destroyer pounding the waves towards him. E-9 sank once more into the sea as the destroyer charged overhead, with propellers throbbing. Horton stayed down until the following evening when he surfaced again into a deserted sea. The crew drank in the clean, fresh air while the boat's batteries were recharged.

Refreshed at last, Horton made for Libau; but when he got there he discovered that it had been put out of action and rendered useless by the enemy. Another base had to be found. Joining up with Laurence, the two British submarines moved to the port of Reval at the western mouth of the Gulf of Finland where they came under the direct command of the Russian Commander-in-Chief of the Baltic Fleet.

Submarine operations, and indeed all naval operations, in that region were restricted because the Gulf froze over during the winter months. Furthermore, since the Germans now knew of the British presence in the Baltic, they withdrew their major warship out of the potentially dangerous waters and left only destroyers to hunt out the submarines and carry out patrols. This denied E-1 and E-9 the targets they had been sent there to hit; but there were other roles in store for them. Initially they reverted to their original task, at the outset of war, of reconnaissance missions into enemy-held harbours, such as Danzig; and as a result of these forays they accumulated much information which was to prove of vital importance to the Russians.

Both Laurence and Horton were anxious to get back on the offensive. But it seemed that they were to be denied the opportunity of sinking any German ships because the area was caught in the grip of winter. The waters began to freeze and if one last mission were not carried out soon, there would be a long wait until the thaw of spring; and nothing frustrates a submariner more than the boredom of waiting and doing nothing.

Horton decided to have a final crack at the enemy before the freeze-up was complete and using an ice-breaker to clear a channel for him he struck out of the Gulf.

Almost a week had passed after his break-out into the Baltic before Horton got the chance he had been waiting for. He had searched the coasts of the Baltic countries without spotting a single worthy target, then on 29 January 1915, while he lay in wait off Moens Klint, at the south-eastern point of Sweden, he sighted three German destroyers coming his way. Alas, they were cruising at full speed and sailing a zig-zag course. They were too difficult targets for him so he reluctantly refrained from attempting an attack.

But then, about an hour later, a single German destroyer ventured towards where he lay, and this time there was no hesitation. He loosed off a single torpedo at a range of 700 yards then took E-9 down and waited. Then a resounding explosion shook the boat. The destroyer had literally been blown to bits by Horton's 'fish'. When he brought E-9 to the surface there was nothing left of the enemy ship. His torpedo must have found her magazine.

Horton had achieved his aim: to strike a blow before naval actions halted for the winter; but his return trip to base was to be infinitely more difficult than he imagined. When he surfaced that evening to recharge his batteries he encountered the full force of the Baltic winter blast. The wind swept across the water casting up on to the bridge spray, which immediately froze, forming a coat of ice inches thick. The ice formed so quickly that crewmen armed with chisels had to chip it away continually.

Horton headed back for Reval but was obliged to dive from time to time in order to melt off the tons of ice which continually formed on the boat's deck, upper casing and conning tower. At last Reval was reached and E-9 was welcomed with enthusiasm following her success; but winter had set in properly and it was to be almost three months later before the British submarines were able to venture out into the Baltic once more.

By then the German army was making substantial advances along the Latvian coast with heavy warships in support, carrying out bombardments and ferrying troops into forward areas. This was the chance the British submarines had been waiting for. At last the Germans were bringing their bigger warships out into action and these made worthwhile targets for the

British torpedoes, even if they were decidedly fickle weapons, occasionally given to performing all sorts of strange antics when they had been fired.

Horton, by now promoted to the rank of commander, had good cause to curse the unreliability and ineffectiveness of the torpedoes with which his boat was armed. Missed opportunities were commonplace as a direct result of faulty torpedoes or impotent explosive charges, as Horton had already discovered to his frustration. It was to be only by sheer determination and an unwillingness to give up that he achieved any success at all with the sub-standard weapons provided.

The British submarine commanders' resolution was paying dividends though, despite the myriad difficulties facing them. Indeed the German C-in-C Baltic, Prince Henry of Russia, was under the impression that the British were operating a *whole flotilla* of submarines in the Baltic. The measure of his concern about British submarine activities in that area is perhaps best illustrated by the address he gave to his U-boat commanders operating in the Baltic. He said:

'I consider the destruction of a Russian submarine will be a great success, but I regard the destruction of a British submarine as being at least as valuable as that of a Russian armoured cruiser.'

Early in May 1915 the port of Libau fell to the advancing Germans and the enemy began reinforcing the area with troops and supplies carried in transports along the coast from Danzig. These transports and their escorting cruisers were to be the targets for Horton. Alas, Laurence could not join in on the sorties for he suffered severe mechanical trouble and had to withdraw to base for lengthy repairs.

While patrolling off the coast, Horton sighted three enemy transports escorted by three cruisers and a cluster of destroyers, forming an outer defensive screen around the convoy. The target was a rich, but difficult one, and would, Horton quickly realized, require all his skill to bring off a 'kill'. He brought E-9 to her full submerged speed of nine knots and dived deep under the destroyer screen; once inside the net, he rose to periscope depth and selected his target, then read off the range, speed and deflection. Moments later the order to fire came and two torpedoes shot away from the submarine. The torpedoes were clearly seen by the Germans and both of them missed their target by some 100 yards. However, undeterred by the fact that his position was now known, Horton brought the boat round and loosed his torpedo from the port-beam tube at the leading transport.

The torpedo ran true from a dangerously close range of only 200 yards. But as it neared the transport it dipped and sped harmlessly beneath it. Horton cursed his luck. By then the destroyers were scurrying about, hunting out the submarine, which was no difficult task; for every time Horton brought her to periscope depth, the periscope cast up a spray which was easily visible to the German lookouts, and the destroyers homed in on E-9 for the kill.

In spite of the impending danger, Horton resolved to continue the attack and swung his boat around, firing a torpedo from the stern tube. This time there was no mistake and it hit the ship square amidships with an explosion that reverberated through the sea to reach the submarine. But already the destroyers were almost on top of E-9 and Horton took her deep. As he did so, the torpedo crew reloaded the tubes. Horton was not satisfied that the job had been finished and was determined to strike again.

With the tubes reloaded Horton brought E-9 up towards the surface, but as he did so the boat was rocked by explosions. The destroyers which were hunting for him began an explosive sweep of the area, using charges dragged behind them. The waters there became decidedly unhealthy and Horton wisely lay low until the noise of the destroyers' propellers had died away. He brought E-9 to periscope depth and found the crippled transport limping through the waves. Hardly daring to breathe, Horton quickly fired a torpedo which hit the transport in the bows. Now she was finished completely and with the job satisfactorily concluded, Horton headed back to base.

Horton's stay back at base was short. His was the only serviceable British submarine and therefore the only one capable of maintaining an offensive in the Baltic. The Russian submarines were vastly inferior and could be virtually discounted as an offensive fighting force. Horton lived up to his responsibilities and reached his peak the following month, June, when he achieved his greatest success to date.

The problem of maintaining the submarines – without proper spares and a suitable depot ship manned by skilled engineers and equipped with servicing equipment – was a constant headache both to Horton and Laurence. The crews of the submarines found themselves carrying out repairs and using all their inventive powers to keep their boats in working order. At the beginning of June, E-9 was in the floating dock at Reval where work was being carried out to repair a fractured propeller shaft. At mid-day on 4 June, Horton got news that a powerful German naval force was steaming west of the Gulf of Riga. This was too good an opportunity to miss, and it stands as a testimony to the ingenuity and labour of the crew that the boat was got ready to put to sea by 5 o'clock that afternoon.

Horton set course to intercept the German force; but while on his way, his wireless operator intercepted a message reporting that the Russian minelayer *Yenisei* had been torpedoed by a U-boat. E-9 dashed to the scene of the incident and found the U-boat still there. Horton had ideas of launching an attack on it but when he dived to begin the attack, the U-boat merely did the same thing and neither boat was in a position to attack. So both had to give up thoughts of sinking the other. They had reached an *impasse* and Horton resumed course for the German surface force.

A few hours later, on the bridge of E-9, Horton sighted plumes of smoke on the horizon that forewarned him of the approach of the German naval force. As they drew closer, he could make out a light cruiser, four destroyers and a collier; altogether a small enemy squadron but a worthwhile target. Then there occurred one of those pieces of luck that come rarely for the submarine commander. Two of the destroyers drew alongside the collier and, with engines stopped, began to take on coal. The three ships became sitting targets and too good to miss.

The cruiser was the most worthwhile prize of the lot though, and Horton devised an attack plan which, if it came off, would net him a formidable bag. Watching from afar, he saw that the cruiser and the two other destroyers were patrolling round the stationary ships, acting as a screen against attack while the refuelling got under way. But Horton thought he could put this to his advantage. He manoeuvred into attack position and waited for the cruiser to sweep into a position almost directly between E-9 and the stationary ships, then he fired a torpedo from his port-beam tube and seconds later two more torpedoes left E-9 aimed at the collier, sitting squat in the water between the destroyers.

Horton's first torpedo capriciously porpoised out of the water and was spotted by the cruiser which managed to avoid it. The prime target had been missed but the other two 'fish' met with better fortune and slammed into the collier, blasting both her and one of the destroyers lying alongside her. Both ships heeled over and sank; but in the meantime, the others had spotted Horton's position and a destroyer was darting towards the submarine, its bows like a knife-edge carving through the water, bent on ramming the boat. Horton, realizing his plight, went deep and narrowly avoided the guillotine.

Later he brought E-9 up and surveyed the scene. Both the collier and the destroyer were gone and the cruiser was busily retrieving survivors from the sea. He had to be content with his day's work and left the scene. Although he had failed to catch the top prize, Horton's actions that day had a substantial effect upon German naval support operations; and these were all but stopped, for a short period at least. This denied the German armies the support they had enjoyed during their advance.

Horton had one near encounter later that month when two German cruisers, escorted by destroyers, made a foray into the Baltic; but by then the German commanders were taking no chances and sailed wild zig-zag patterns. When Horton set himself up for an attack, the squadron suddenly changed course away from him and sped off, and he lost the chance of increasing his score.

For the last few days of the month, weather conditions in the Baltic changed dramatically and a thick blanket of fog lay over the area where the German ships were likely to operate, in Horton's patrol. So dense was the fog that Horton encountered great difficulty in navigating, and felt his way along the shallow waters of the coastline by running the submarine submerged towards the shore until it grounded in 8 fathoms of water; a dangerous but seemingly effective method of taking soundings!

On 2 July the fog cleared, and Horton had no sooner surfaced when he sighted another German cruiser squadron, comprising two cruisers and a protecting group of destroyers. Down he went and headed to attack at full speed. Firing from 400 yards, Horton sent two torpedoes thudding into the side of the armoured cruiser *Prinz Adalbert*. Both exploded with ear-rendering blasts, severely damaging the warship; but now Horton found himself in a perilous position. The fine trimming of the submarine had been upset by the exit of the torpedoes and E-9 shot on to the surface where she was immediately spotted by an escorting destroyer which raced towards her, bent on ramming. Only the combined skill of E-9's crew saved her from destruction when they crash-dived to the bottom; stopping when she dug her nose into the mud. Horton threw his engines into reverse and she bobbed clear of the mud and high-tailed it away, leaving behind a badly damaged cruiser.

Had Horton's torpedoes been more powerful, the *Prinz Adalbert* would have sunk but they were like pinpricks in the heavily armoured cruiser. Horton had, however, achieved a signal success, for the cruiser had to limp back to base and spent several months there undergoing repairs when she might otherwise have been employed in aiding the advance of the German armies. Indeed, so important was this success that Horton was decorated with Russia's highest military award, the Order of St George.

The degree of success enjoyed by Horton, and to a lesser extent Laurence, found acclaim not only in Russia but also in Britain, where the Admiralty decided to reinforce the Baltic Flotilla with more E-class submarines and some of the smaller C-class types. The plan to build up the flotilla was an ambitious one. Four E-class submarines were given the task of negotiating the treacherous Sound, through which E-1 and E-9 had already passed. Remembering E-9's difficulty made the mission all the more hazardous. Four C-class submarines, it was planned, would reach the Baltic in a more novel manner. They were to be towed to Archangel then loaded on to barges and transported to the Baltic by way of a cobweb system of canals. This part of the operation was actually completed, thanks in no small part to the ingenuity and labours of the Russian bargees. But it hit a problem.

To lighten the load, it was decided that the C-class boats would be stripped of their batteries in England and these would be sent to Russia in a transport ship. Alas, on its way, this ship was torpedoed and sunk, so this left four perfectly good submarines in the Baltic incapable of going into action. It was to take many months before replacement batteries eventually reached them and they were able to go into action.

As for the E-class boats, theirs was a much more hazardous passage. It was the intention that they would proceed from England, slip through the Sound and rendezvous with Horton's E-9 in the Gulf of Finland. Four of them set off, E-8 (Lieutenant Commander Goodhart); E-13 (Lieutenant Commander Layton); E-18 (Lieutenant Commander Halahan); and E-19 (Lieutenant Commander Cromie). All of them succeeded in getting through the notorious Sound but one of them, the E-13, was destined to have a short life in the Baltic.

Disaster struck the ill-fated boat shortly after Layton had successfully brought her through the Sound, when her magnetic compass failed to function and she went wildly off course and ran aground on a mud-bank inside Danish territorial waters. Layton found himself in a decidedly awkward position for, under the rules of International Law, a warship could remain in neutral waters for only twenty-four hours and, try as they might, E-13's crew could not unstick her from the mud or even lighten her sufficiently so that she might float clear at high tide.

The penalty for remaining inside territorial waters over the allowed twenty-four hour period was internment and this was a fate that Layton obviously wanted to avoid at all cost. All on board laboured throughout the night in a bid to free her but they did so in vain. At 5 a.m. a Danish destroyer closed in to keep watch and remind Layton that his time was running out. It was at about that time that two other ships came into sight, bu these had more belligerent intentions. They were German torpedo boats and contrary to all the rules laid down under International Law and completely oblivious to the Danish destroyer, their commander launched a torpedo at the grounded submarine. Luckily the German 'fish' missed E-13 but slammed into the mud beneath her and exploded. The explosion was enormous but did little or no damage to the submarine. Seeing that his torpedo had failed to achieve its aim, the German commander then closed in and opened fire on E-13 with his guns. E-13 had no defence against such an attack and almost instantly was transformed into a blazing wreck. Already several of her crew were dead or injured and seeing that the Germans had no intentions of letting up in their barbaric attack, Layton gave the order to abandon ship. But even then, the Germans continued to rake them with fire, killing more of them.

On board the Danish destroyer which by law was not at liberty to open fire, her captain could hardly believe the audacity and savagery of the attack. In a bid to save the remainder of the men in the water, he gallantly brought his ship to a position between the blazing submarine and the German torpedo boats. Of E-13's entire crew, only sixteen survived, including Layton. They were taken aboard the Danish destroyer and put into internment but were repatriated before the end of the war.

The presence of the British submarines in the Baltic was a thorn in the side of the German Navy and plans were afoot to destroy their base at Riga. Only hours after the cowardly destruction of E-13 a powerful German naval force cruised for Riga, bent on bombarding it to destruction. Forewarned of their approach, Laurence and Horton left the port to do what they could to stop the advancing squadron. It fell to Laurence to gain distinction that day when, after sighting the approaching squadron, he fired two torpedoes at the battle-cruiser *Moltke* and damaged her. Admiral von Hipper, commanding the squadron, was so shaken by the attack that he called off the mission and took his ships back to harbour. The port of Riga was saved and Laurence was accorded the same honour previously received by Horton, the Order of St George.

From then on, with the increased submarine force in the Baltic, attacks began with a vengeance upon merchantmen carrying the vital iron ore from Sweden to Germany's war factories. Goodhart in E-8 was the first to draw blood when he sank the steamer *Margarette* as she left Königsberg. In accordance with prize rules, she was first stopped, searched to ensure that she was carrying 'contraband', then sunk by gunfire after her crew had been allowed to take to the boats.

Goodhart was to achieve a noteworthy 'double' on that patrol when, off Libau, he sighted the cruiser *Prinz Adalbert*, out of port for the first time following repairs after being damaged by Horton. With her were two destroyers. Goodhart dived underneath the destroyer screen and from a range of 1,300 yards fired a single torpedo at the *Prinz Adalbert*. It ran true and caught her in the fore magazine. Even at her extreme range, the submarine was rocked by the resulting explosion and when, a few minutes later, Goodhart brought her to periscope depth, there was no sign of the cruiser. He had finished what Horton had begun.

This successful day's shooting started the ball rolling for the other submarines and it was Cromie in E-19 who had a field day on 11 October. He sank no fewer than *five* merchantmen in fairly quick succession without the loss of a single life. So devastating was the effect of these victories that the shipping of iron ore from Sweden was temporarily stopped until convoy protection could be arranged. The 'protection' given comprised two cruisers and two flotillas of destroyers; but the diversion of these units for convoy protection meant that other large German warships had to stay at home, for they dared not leave port without supporting destroyers. Cromie's one-day patrol had paid handsome dividends and given the German Naval High Command a king-size headache.

The following month, Cromie earned further laurels when he sank the 2,650-ton cruiser *Undine* in a daring attack. Having crippled her with one torpedo, he was not satisfied that he had dealt her a mortal blow and was determined to make sure. Although the ship was already beginning to sink slowly, he took E-19 beneath her stern and fired another torpedo into her, blowing her to bits. Then, content that he'd done a good job, he left the scene and an escorting destroyer picked up survivors.

Towards the end of November all the submarines returned to their base for the winter, when operations had to cease over the freezing months. It was then that the Admiralty ordered Horton and Laurence back to Britain. At this the Russians were little short of furious. Horton in particular had found a special place in the hearts of the Russians. They held him in very high regard and indeed requested that he should remain in the Baltic as the Senior Submarine Officer. The Admiralty, however, would not have it and insisted upon his return.

Before he left Baltic shores, he was given a send-off the like of which had rarely – if ever before – been accorded a British naval officer by the Russians.

The remainder of the time spent by British submarines in the Baltic was, by comparison, uneventful. With the Germans' tightening up of their convoy system, targets not only became scarcer but very much more difficult to attack. These two factors, coupled with the introduction of the depth charge, denied the submarine commanders the spectacular success enjoyed by their predecessors, Laurence and Horton. Cromie, now the Senior Naval Officer Baltic, found that the small C-class submarines, which by then had been equipped with fresh batteries from England, were less potent against the strengthened German convoys.

British submarine activities in the Baltic came to a sad end in 1917 when, following the Russian Revolution, Cromie was obliged to scuttle all his boats rather than allow them to fall into the hands of the Reds, who had signed an Armistice with Germany and agreed to hand over all British submarines to them. This was a situation which Cromie could not tolerate and one day in November 1917, he took his flotilla to sea and sent his boats to the bottom with the use of explosive charges. So ended the Baltic campaign.

The Marmara

There were those who were sceptical about the worth of the submarine as a weapon of war, but that scepticism was to be for ever swept away when a handful of submariners went into action in another landlocked sea, the Marmara. This is a very much smaller spread of water than the Baltic but one in which the British Submarine Service truly won its spurs – and a string of Victoria Crosses.

The stories of courage and daring shown by British submariners in this theatre of war are legion and recounting them all would take more than one volume. The exploits of those submarine commanders who won the Victoria Cross during the campaign against the Turks epitomizes the kind of courage which was shown to a man in that bloody campaign.

Danger was an ever-present and unwelcome companion for the submariner who ventured through the narrow, shallow and heavily defended Dardanelles into the Sea of Marmara where, shortly after the beginning of the First World War, lay two German warships, the *Goeben*, a battle-cruiser, and the *Breslau*, a light cruiser. These two powerful warships sought refuge from the British Fleet in the Sea of Marmara and were handed over to the Turks by the Germans to strengthen a weak and inefficient Turkish fleet. Allied intelligence was well aware, however, that although these ships were ostensibly now part of the Turkish Navy, they were, in fact, still manned by German seamen and therefore legitimate targets for the British Fleet.

At the outbreak of war in August 1914, Turkey was neutral and therefore British or Allied warships were prohibited entry to the Marmara by way of the Turkish waters of the Dardanelles. This may have given those aboard the two warships a sense of security but any feeling of immunity they might have felt was to be swiftly removed in a gallant action by one of Britain's oldest submarines.

The first British submarines, along with some French boats, arrived at Moudhros on the island of Limnos in August 1914 to take up station in the Aegean Sea. They were B-9, 10 and 11 along with the French *Circe, Coulomb, Faraday* and *Le Verrier,* and they had with them the converted merchantman *Hindu Kush* which was to act as a depot ship.

By comparison with the E-class boats, all of these were 'antiques'. The B-class boats, built around 1907, were small craft used primarily for coastal work. They had a surface displacement of 285 tons and length of about 143 feet. Surface power was derived from a petrol engine, a motive power which was bedevilled with problems because of its lethal fumes and tendency to catch fire. This engine produced a surface speed of 12 knots while the battery-fed electric motor managed a maximum submerged speed of some $6\frac{1}{2}$ knots for the limited period of one hour.

Conditions on board were indescribably bad. The air was constantly tinged with the heavy petrol fumes off the engine which produced headaches for the crew who were obliged to eat, sleep and go into action in the severely cramped space afforded them among the maze of pipes and other equipment. But, if that were not enough, the boat itself was a decidedly difficult craft to handle, a poor runner on the surface and a sluggish and uneasy boat to handle submerged.

This then was the 'weapon' with which the British submariners were to wage war. Winston Churchill, then First Lord of the Admiralty, ordered them to '... sink *Goeben* and *Breslau,* no matter what flag they fly if they come out of the Dardanelles...'

British submarines kept up a constant patrol at the mouth of the Dardanelles while powerful elements of the Mediterranean Fleet stood sentinel to guard the German warships' exit point into the Aegean. Then in October, the Ottoman Empire declared its true colours and sided with the Central Powers. The gloves were off. No longer were there the niceties of neutral treaty to consider. The time had come for the submarines to go into action, but to do so they would have to venture into the Turkish lair, the Sea of Marmara.

To understand the enormity of the problem presenting itself to Lieutenant Commander Pownall, the Commander (Submarines), when he planned the penetration of the Dardanelles, there were two factors to appreciate. The first was the strength of the Turkish defences along the Narrows, the middle section of the strip of water that links the Marmara with the Aegean. The second was the short submersible endurance of his submarines, which could not undertake the full voyage in a submerged attitude. Both banks of the Narrows were bristling with guns and searchlights which played on the water throughout the hours of darkness.

Time, however, had not allowed the Turks to lay impenetrable anti-submarine nets and mines in these Narrows – these were to come later – but there was a considerable barrier of five rows of moored mines through which an Allied submarine would have to find its way before reaching the Sea. Furthermore the Turks had Nature on their side because there were strong currents in the Narrows and a layer of fresh water which could spell doom for the unwary submariner in that, because of its less buoyant property, it could instantly upset a boat's trim and send her to the bottom.

Despite these many difficulties, Pownall decided to send a submarine into the Narrows to determine whether or not a passage was possible. Lieutenant Norman Holbrook was chosen to undertake the task in his submarine B-11, and 13 December found him running on the surface into the Dardanelles Straits. From the bridge he could see ahead of him the Turks' searchlights sweeping the waters of the Narrows and he opted to dive and lie deep to wait for the half-light of dawn before making his attempt.

B-11 had been specially converted for this sortie with the addition of tubular steel guards which fitted over the protuberances on the submarine. This would, it was hoped, allow it to run through the minefield by pushing aside the mine cables as it went.

As the first light of dawn came, Holbrook brought B-11 to the surface and slipped towards the entrance to the Dardanelles opposite Cape Helles, then he trimmed down and nosed into Turkish waters. B-11's electric motor pushed her along at a bare two knots as Holbrook felt his way deeper into the Straits at a depth of eighty feet. But as he did so, all on board became aware of a persistent vibration which seemed to be coming from outside the casing. They racked their brains to figure out what it could be but none could come up with a satisfactory explanation.

Worried that it might be something serious which could endanger the success of their mission, Holbrook decided to take a chance and surface to have a look. He brought B-11 up and scrambled on to the deck where he found the cause of the trouble. One of the specially fitted tubular guards had worked loose and was rattling against the steel casing. Holbrook ordered two seamen on to the deck and, flexing their muscles, they hauled it off and tossed it into the sea.

Wasting no time, B-11 was taken down once more and resumed course again. By then daylight was almost upon the Dardanelles and to linger a moment longer would certainly have resulted in detection, which would inevitably have meant the end of the mission.

On the submarine went, and it succeeded in penetrating the minefields without event. Then, just before 10 a.m., Holbrook brought B-11 to periscope depth and to his delight found the old Turkish battleship *Messudieh* sitting plump and resplendent at anchor off his starboard beam. This was a target not to be missed, and Holbrook swiftly gave the preparatory orders that brought the boat round and nosing against the strong current to an attacking position, 800 yards from the motionless battleship.

Both forward tubes were flooded as an air of tense expectancy rose to a high pitch throughout the length of the boat. Holbrook manoeuvred his boat into the firing position, warding off the excitement that was growing in him as he gave the last corrections to course. All was ready and everyone waited, poised for his order. The *Messudieh* lay square in the hairlines of the periscope's lens and Holbrook uttered the words:

'Fire both!'

B-11 recoiled slightly as the two bow torpedoes raced out of their tubes. But as they did so the trim of the boat was slightly upset and for the crucial moment of impact Holbrook's view was obscured as the periscope's eye dipped underwater. However, seen or not, there was no doubt about their accuracy. The two torpedoes hit the target square, and exploded. Almost instantly the battleship began to sink at the stern as a gaping hole in her side gulped in tons of water.

But the Turks on board had been momentarily forewarned of their fate after sighting the twin trails of bubbles in the water, and dashed to action stations. Already their guns were firing and shells thrashed the water around B-11. These were joined by batteries on the shore which opened up at the sub-

31

marine's position with frightening accuracy. Holbrook took
B-11 into the depths and swung her round so that her bows
were set towards his exit from the Straits. As he did so, the
Messudieh capsized, entombing the Turks who had held their
posts on her. Luckily for them many were not killed when she
overturned and, the next day, engineers succeeded in cutting
holes in her keel through which the Turks were able to escape.

Right up to the point of attack and for a few moments after
it, Holbrook had enjoyed a comparatively uneventful voyage;
but now the tables were to turn on him and escape from the
danger area was to be fraught with problems. The first of these
was spotted by Lieutenant Winn, the First Lieutenant, when
he tried to take a compass reading and found that the lens was
fogged up. The compass of B-11 was mounted on the deck of
the submarine, outside the casing, and could only be viewed
through an arrangement of lenses when the submarine was
underwater. Now that the lens had fogged up, they found themselves having to navigate blind in hostile waters, a singularly
uncomfortable situation to be in and one that was almost certain to have serious consequences. They came almost immediately when the whole submarine shuddered to a halt, grounded
on the bottom in shallow water.

Holbrook threw his motors into full power and B-11 thrashed
her way off the mud into deeper water, only to run aground
once more, but this time more firmly stuck. Now there was an
added problem when Holbrook discovered that the conning
tower of the submarine must be showing above the water, sticking up like a sore thumb for all to see. The first to spot it were
the Turkish gunners on shore, and they opened up with a
vengeance.

Their situation was perilous in the extreme as the shell-
bursts crept towards the submarine. Meanwhile Holbrook, oblivious of the rain of shells, concentrated on getting B-11 off
the mud-bank. The electric motors whined at full power as the
propeller gouged out great clods of mud until at last Holbrook's
efforts were rewarded when the submarine eased forward,
gradually gathering speed until she was free of the mud-bank
and able to dive deep to the invisibility of the depths.

Although severely hampered by the useless compass, Holbrook brought that boat through the minefield and back down
the Straits to the safety of the sea and subsequently back to
base, where a tumultuous welcome awaited him and his crew. In

that sortie, Holbrook had severely shaken the Turks, a race not given to nervousness; and as a result of it, he was awarded the Victoria Cross – the first submariner to be so honoured and indeed it was the first VC to be awarded to a naval officer in that war.

Holbrook had drawn first blood, and other equally courageous submariners were to follow suit and perform feats of daring in the Straits and the Marmara.

In spite of Holbrook's success it was realized that the B-class boats were pitifully inadequate for the task designated them and an urgent plea went to the Admiralty from Admiral Carden, who was master-minding the naval operations in the Dardanelles area, to send some E-class boats and reinforce their strength. At first his request had no result because Their Lordships regarded the operations in that area of secondary importance to those taking place in the North Sea and the Baltic. But then there came a turn of events which was to change their minds radically.

A top-level decision was made to bombard the Turkish fortresses at the Dardanelles and use a powerful naval force to break through the Straits, into the Marmara, with the object of taking Constantinople. This plan was conceived and approved on 28 January 1915, and a few days later, Commodore Roger Keyes arrived to take up appointment as Chief-of-Staff to Admiral Carden. Keyes, although not himself a submariner, had been a key figure in the build-up of British submarine strength and an ardent protagonist of its use. Before the outbreak of the war he had been Commodore (Submarines) until taking over command of the Overseas Flotilla. With such a man so close to the 'top management' in the Mediterranean theatre it was clear that submarines were destined to play an important and growing part in operations in that area.

The bombardment of the Turkish forts began in mid-February but the Anglo-French fleet which attempted to force a passage through the Straits was halted by the minefields. The plan was abandoned. It seemed that, in the meantime, the job of disrupting Turkish operations in the Marmara and severing her sea-borne supply lines across it was to fall to the Submarine Service. It was therefore decided to comply with Carden's request for E-class submarines, and the Admiralty released seven of them – together with an Australian submarine – to come under the command of Admiral de Robeck, who had succeeded

Carden following his being invalided home.

Three E-class submarines left England as the advance party of these boats. They were E-11, commanded by Lieutenant Commander Martin Nasmith, who it will be remembered had been denied the opportunity of going to war in the Baltic through mechanical trouble, and two others: E-14 (Lieutenant Commander Courtney Boyle), and E-15 (Lieutenant Commander T. S. Brodie). It was with considerable optimism that they set out for Moudhros, but again Nasmith was to suffer mechanical trouble when a main shaft fractured and he limped into Malta behind the other two. There he learned that he would be delayed, since another shaft would have to be shipped out from England.

Disappointed, but not totally disheartened, Nasmith spent much of his time in Malta pondering on the problem of forcing a way through the Straits into the Marmara. Eventually, after Boyle and Brodie had left Malta, impatience got the better of him and he decided to set sail for Moudhros after only temporary repairs had been completed. He still had a cracked shaft but Nasmith was determined that, come what may, he would not be denied a fight twice.

But when Nasmith at last reached the new depot ship *Adamant* at Moudhros he was dealt a bitter blow. He learned that Brodie in E-15 had already made the attempt to reach the Marmara; an attempt that resulted in disaster. E-15 was swept into the shore and stuck on a mud-bank where she came under the fire of the Turkish shore guns. One of the first shells hit the conning tower just as Brodie was emerging and he was killed instantly. Nothing the remainder of the crew did could move E-15 off the mud and a torpedo boat was closing in fast. Then a shell blasted through the hull and shattered one of the batteries, filling the whole submarine with lethal chlorine gas. The crew had no choice but to surrender.

Royal Naval Air Service aircraft flying overhead witnessed the tragic incident and reported back to base what had happened, and also that attempts were being made by the Turks to salvage the crippled boat. This was something that could not be allowed to happen, and the Royal Navy went to extraordinary lengths to sink their own boat. She was attacked from the air and bombarded from the sea, as well as attacked by a B-class submarine whose two torpedoes missed. Finally the Navy sent in two picket boats armed with torpedoes and in a daring attack at night one of them torpedoed the E-15 which was blown out of the water. The other picket boat was hit squarely by a Turkish shell and sunk.

After this attack it seemed that the job had been successfully concluded but there was still some doubt as to whether or not the submarine had been irretrievably sunk and that the secret equipment and documents she contained were safe from the Turks. Confirmation had to be sought, and a B-class submarine was sent in to have a closer look at her. In so doing, however, she almost suffered a similar fate when, caught by the same swift current which had thrust E-15 on to the bank, she landed high and almost dry on the same bank. Thanks to some timely advice given to her commander by Lieutenant Commander C. G. Brodie, the twin brother of the unfortunate E-15's commander, he managed to squirm clear and beat a retreat but not before finding that E-15 was well and truly sunk beyond possible salvage.

The efforts made to ensure the destruction of E-15 were hailed not only by the British but also by the Turks and the Germans who had witnessed the heroism shown by those who took part.

Despite the tragedy, there was an eagerness among the other submarine commanders to have a crack at getting through the Straits, but a temporary halt was made to such operations. Then came one of the bloodiest battles in the annals of war: the landings at Gallipoli. The military force designated the task of landing on the sandy beaches and taking Gallipoli was largely composed of Australian and New Zealand troops and it was coincidental that it was the Australian submarine AE-2 which was given orders to attempt a penetration of the Straits.

As the landing got under way and the wholesale slaughter began, Lieutenant Commander Stoker took AE-2 into the Straits, through the minefields under the very noses of the Turks and into the Sea of Marmara. In a voyage which passed without major event; Stoker had pulled it off where others had so tragically failed. Now he was at large in the Turks' haven and hunting for prey.

The news of Stoker's success was greeted with joy both by the military and naval commanders, and it was largely because of its presence there and the belief that Stoker could arrest the flow of supply traffic across the Marmara that it was decided to continue with the landings and fight it out, in spite of almost catastrophic reverses on the beaches. Had AE-2 not succeeded in forcing a passage through the Straits then perhaps the military commanders might have had the sense to pull out their troops when it became clear that the operation was turning into a bloodbath. They grossly over-estimated the potential damage a single submarine could inflict. The result of this tragic decision was a casualty list in excess of 100,000 which tore the heart out of the ANZAC forces and from then on gave the name Gallipoli a new and terrible meaning.

The tragedy of Gallipoli was made all the more awful when AE-2 failed to sink a single enemy ship and, following an encounter with a Turkish torpedo boat, was forced to scuttle with the loss of some of her crew and the capture of Stoker and nineteen of his men; a sad end to the successful penetration of what were perhaps the most difficult waters in any theatre of war. Had it not been for Lieutenant Commander Courtney Boyle the whole débâcle might have been total.

The day following Stoker's entry into the Marmara, Boyle repeated the success in E-14; but even this was marred by the news that the French submarine *Joule* was lost with all hands in a similar bid. But at least Boyle was through and determined to bring destruction upon the Turkish ships – and this he did. His first 'kill' came on 10 May when he sent the 5,000-ton transport ship *Gul Djemal* to the bottom. This might not on the face of it have been such a marvellous achievement had it not been for the fact that she was carrying 6,000 Turkish troops.

However, in sinking the *Gul Djemal* Boyle had expended his last torpedo, having used all his others in unsuccessful attacks. Typical of the man, though, he remained in the Marmara, stopping and searching Turkish ships and on one occasion actually forcing a steamer to run aground. This feat was all the more remarkable when one considers that his sole armament was a handful of rifles. In spite of these rather novel successes, it was clear that E-14 was wasted in the Marmara without a supply of torpedoes and she was ordered back to base. Now Boyle had to repeat his successful passage through the Straits, but this time in reverse – and this he did to an unrivalled welcome, promotion to the rank of commander and the subsequent award of the Victoria Cross for his daring.

By the time of Boyle's return, Nasmith's E-11 had been fitted with her new shaft and was ready for operational duties; and now it was his turn to 'run amuck in the Marmara', as Roger

Keyes put it. As we shall see, Nasmith was to emerge the supreme champion of the submariners in the Marmara and it is fitting that it is his story that is told in greater detail, for it illustrates the courage and resource shown by his fellow commanders in the desperate struggle against the Turks.

Before setting off in E-11 to force the Straits, Nasmith took the unprecedented step of carrying out a personal aerial reconnaissance of the stretch of water in an old Maurice Farman biplane. He was taking no chances and was determined to ensure that he knew every inch of these treacherous waters before he tried to force a passage through. It was as well that he did, for his run through the Straits was to be charged with danger and near-catastrophe.

E-11 stood to sea on 19 May escorted by the destroyer *Grasshopper* until some four miles up the Straits when the destroyer swept away, leaving Nasmith and E-11 alone in these hostile waters.

Nasmith took his boat down and inched his way forward through the aquarian forest of mine cables while the Turkish searchlights played on the water's surface and the defending gunners stood to their posts, their eyes tracing the pools of light on the rippling water for the slightest hint of an intruder; but E-11 went undetected. That is, until Nasmith brought her to periscope depth when he reached deeper water. He was spotted instantly and the guns blazed into life, hurtling shells at the slender shadow that slipped along only feet beneath the surface. The Turks' aim was good – too good to linger, and Nasmith took E-11 down into the sanctuary of the deep and proceeded through the Narrows until finally he slid through the last triple row of mines. The moment he had been denied for so long was here. Nasmith was in the Marmara at last and, fighting off the urge to launch himself straight into the fray, he took E-11 down to the bottom where she remained for the day.

By evening the foul stench in the boat was becoming unbearable and Nasmith could plainly see that his crew was suffering from advanced oxygen starvation. At 9 p.m. he decided to bring E-11 to the surface and the hatches were thrown open. An almost instant resurgence of enthusiasm resulted from the intake of clean air but E-11 could not remain on the surface without danger. Twice enemy destroyers hove into sight and Nasmith was obliged to take his boat down quickly, but he reckoned that he had not been seen.

The following day Nasmith got down to work and began patrolling off the mouth of the Straits, but the sea was empty and, even when he moved position in the afternoon, there was still no sign of enemy naval activity. Bored by the inactivity, Nasmith decided the time had come for some relaxation, and in spite of the many dangers around him, he allowed his crew to take a 'dip' in the Marmara.

That night, E-11 recharged her batteries on the surface and the following morning she patrolled again but without sighting any ship; so again, Nasmith allowed his crew to take a swim before getting under way once more.

Nasmith, never a man to miss an opportunity and a master of the art of improvisation, seized a chance of devising a ruse. He sighted a two-masted schooner and sent a boarding party aboard her. She was found to be carrying logs but it was not her cargo that interested Nasmith so much as her two tall masts. These, he thought, would make ideal lookout posts for him. The short conning tower of the E-class submarine was far from ideal as a lookout point but the towering masts of a schooner were near perfect, so he ordered Lieutenant D'Oyly Hughes to take command of her with a man perched at her mast-head while the sails were set, and she got under way with E-11 sliding in her shadow, out of view of enemy ships. What captain, Nasmith pondered, would suspect the presence of a British submarine so close to an innocent schooner? It was a clever trick but it paid no dividends, and he eventually allowed the schooner to go unmolested.

On the morning of 23 May E-11 slid through the water towards the Ottoman capital of Constantinople and it was here, after nosing around for some time, spying out the lay of the land, that Nasmith made his first strike. E-11 had got right up to the harbour mouth and there Nasmith found a Turkish torpedo gunboat lying at anchor. From 700 yards he sent a torpedo smack into her, amidships. Almost immediately the boat began to sink but in spite of a heavy list to starboard the guns crew closed up and fired at Nasmith's periscope. The first shot missed but the second, by some fluke or eagle eye, hit the periscope and bored a neat hole in it, leaving it standing almost by a thread. With that kind of luck on the side of the Turks, Nasmith was not fool enough to hang around, and he beat an underwater retreat to a safe position where he surfaced to remove the damaged periscope and reload the empty torpedo tube.

Nasmith's cruise on the Marmara was nothing if it was not crowded with unusual incidents. The night following the sinking of the Turkish boat, Nasmith made contact with his base, having previously encountered difficulty in doing so, and at last was able to inform them that he had safely arrived in the Marmara.

At 6 a.m., E-11 set off on patrol again and sighted the *Nagara*, a small steamer which Nasmith brought to a halt for inspection. The sight of the submarine brought panic aboard her and crew and passengers alike made a frantic rush for the lifeboats. But amid this chaos, a man appeared at the ship's rail and in a strong American accent boldly introduced himself to Nasmith as Raymond Swing, a reporter of the *Chicago Herald*, whereupon he asked Nasmith if he could give him a story! The situation was comic to say the least but Nasmith, remembering his duty, was more interested in the cargo the steamer was carrying. Swing obligingly gave him the details, informing him that she was loaded with guns and ammunition and was transporting a detachment of Marines.

Having got the information he wanted Nasmith advised Swing to find a lifeboat and get aboard as quickly as possible for in a few minutes he would be blasting the ship to 'kingdom come'. This he did until nothing remained of the *Nagara* save its lifeboats filled with its crew and passengers.

It was then that Nasmith sighted yet another steamer leaving the port of Rodosto, and he turned on her. But by then the violent explosion of *Nagara* had forewarned her captain that danger lurked and he turned tail and put back into port, mooring alongside a pier where the crew leapt off her. Nasmith, determined to get a 'double', slid in so close to the shore that E-11 scraped the bottom of the shallows, then he fired. There was a tremendous explosion in which the steamer all but disappeared, taking with it most of the pier. She too had been carrying ammunition.

Nasmith withdrew, but as he was doing so he sighted another target, this time a paddle-steamer. He couldn't believe his luck for she looked like a worthwhile target to make a likely hat-trick.

The paddle-steamer was heading in for the harbour when Nasmith surfaced and ordered her captain to stop; but he wasn't having any of it and turned on E-11 to ram. The steamer narrowly missed E-11 then veered off heading for the shore and steering a zig-zag course. Nasmith, not wanting to waste a torpedo, called on the submarine's sharp-shooters to come to the bridge whereupon they opened up with rifles at the steamer's bridge, scattering the captain and his helmsmen and forcing the steamer to slew wildly about, out of control.

Somehow the helmsman got the steamer under control again and she veered round, bent on ramming the surfaced submarine. Again the sharp-shooters opened up and this time it was too much for the gallant steamer. She swept into the shore and ran aground, whereupon Nasmith ordered D'Oyly Hughes to board her and blow her up. But the first lieutenant was not to achieve his goal. Hughes, with two sailors, rowed over to her and clambered aboard but as they were doing so – the cavalry arrived! A posse of Turkish cavalrymen rode into sight, dismounted and took up positions amid the scrub behind the beach and proceeded to rake the steamer and the submarine with fire to which Nasmith's sharp-shooters replied with a series of volleys. It was clear that Hughes was not to succeed and, under the cover of Nasmith's fire, he and the two seamen got back to the submarine and Nasmith submerged. Frustrated at being denied his target by a handful of horsemen, Nasmith set a torpedo at the steamer but it missed. With that he decided to spare her and made off deep into the Marmara.

Nasmith was bent on returning to Constantinople, the heart of the Ottoman Empire, and striking again. These were shock tactics and the kind in which Nasmith believed. If only he could carry it off, the Turks would be greatly unnerved by the thought that a submarine could at will penetrate the harbour of the capital and run riot in it.

Nasmith and Hughes got their heads together in the wardroom and pored over the charts of the Constantinople harbour and its environs. They quickly appreciated how lucky they had been during their first visit to the harbour. The charts showed only the surface currents prevailing and there were no details of the currents they were likely to encounter beneath the surface. If they were anything like those in the Dardanelles Straits, then they were to have their work cut out for them. But Nasmith, in spite of the possibility of problems in the harbour, was determined to have a go again and on 25 May slipped into the harbour, passing by the coastal small fry which didn't merit a torpedo. Once within the confines of the harbour Nasmith set about finding a target and was not long in sighting one, the transport *Stamboul*.

With practised precision, Nasmith went through the attack procedure, lining up E-11 for a straight shot. Then he fired a bow torpedo which began to perform a frenzied series of antics, leaping in and out of the water and veering around out of control. Nasmith immediately fired his second bow torpedo which found its mark but then he found his maverick torpedo slicing through the water towards E-11 almost on the point of collision; and it was only by some deft manoeuvring of the boat that he avoided being sent to the bottom by his own 'fish'.

By then he had been spotted by the shore batteries and they opened up on him, lashing the water with shell fire and transforming it into a bubbling turmoil. Nasmith took E-11 as deep as he dared but he was caught by one of the criss-cross underwater currents and swept wildly off course, then became grounded on the Leander bank. Luckily for him a quick thrust of power on the motors and she was off it and nosing out of the harbour and well away from trouble.

Nasmith had given the Turks a nasty fright but after the tension of his escapade he decided to give his crew a brief rest to build up their strength once more for the patrols that lay ahead. So the following day was spent well out to sea and in a relaxed state while Nasmith allowed his crew to take turns of bathing. But as they enjoyed the comparatively cool waters, a Turkish plane appeared in the sky above and turned to attack. The alarm was raised and the swimmers were hauled on board while the aircraft dived down on it. Hatches were secured and E-11 plunged beneath the waves – none too soon, for seconds later three bombs hit the water nearby and exploded, luckily without causing any damage. Theirs was a narrow escape and a sharp reminder that vigilance had to be the key word while cruising in the Marmara.

Following the explosions, Nasmith brought E-11 to surface again but the enemy plane had gone and they returned to their respite but keeping an ever-watchful eye on the sky lest some of the aviator's friends should return.

It was to be 27 May before E-11 saw action again and she was presented for the second time with a target which she had attempted to attack while coming through the Dardanelles Straits. It was the battleship *Harridin Barbarossa*. Nasmith manoeuvred into attacking position but the battleship and her attendant destroyers were too fast for her. She was spotted and forced to flee to avoid being rammed by a destroyer.

Nasmith was concerned about his dwindling supply of torpedoes. He had only five left which allowed him no room for misses. From then on every one had to count; which meant making no daring attacks but firing only at sure targets. The following day he found the first of them when he sighted a large steamer escorted by a destroyer, with smaller merchantmen making up a convoy. Nasmith slipped beneath the destroyer and slammed home a torpedo which sank the steamer almost immediately.

Such was Nasmith's concern over conserving his torpedoes that he devised a system of retrieving them if they failed to hit the target. Normally torpedoes are set to sink at the end of their run if they fail to make a hit but D'Oyly Hughes altered the setting so that, if they missed, they would remain on the surface and could be found and brought back on board the boat. Such an operation was tinged with danger for the torpedo would still be 'live' and if carelessly handled would blow the submarine to smithereens.

The day after his successful attack on the steamer, Nasmith brought E-11 towards the mouth of the harbour at Constantinople where he caught sight of a big transport ship crammed with passengers on her decks. Nasmith from the distance of 1,000 yards took the ship to be a military troop carrier and fired a torpedo. Had that torpedo run true instead of veering wildly off course and missing the ship, Nasmith might well have been labelled a murderer and have tarnished a hitherto impeccable record, for the souls on the decks of that ship were women and children being evacuated. Upon realizing this, Nasmith had good cause to be thankful that the gyro-mechanism in the torpedo had failed.

Nasmith watched as the transport steamed past then he surfaced and set about looking for the torpedo, which he found floating in the swell. Not prepared to risk the life of one of his seamen, Nasmith took it upon himself to dive over the side and remove the pistol from the warhead. When he had accomplished this the submarine was trimmed down forward, bringing the stern awash, and the torpedo was brought inboard through the tube.

Nasmith found a good use for that torpedo when on 31 May,

having been informed by radio from base that Turkish ships were gathering in the western Marmara, he slid in towards the port of Panderma and found there a prize target – a transport ship on the point of embarking troops for the front. He loosed a torpedo at her from his port-beam tube and it rammed home, severely damaging her.

The following day Nasmith took E-11 to the north-eastern corner of the Marmara and there found a munitions ship escorted by a destroyer. His torpedo sent her below in only three minutes. Later another steamer was sighted and Nasmith fired at her but missed and the torpedo could not be found. Now he was left with only one torpedo. Some hours later a dispatch vessel hove to and Nasmith fired his last torpedo at it *but it missed*. Luckily he was able to retrieve it and get it back on board again.

It was about then E-11 began to show signs of mechanical trouble, when a crack appeared in one of the intermediate shafts between a diesel engine and its main motor. This, coupled with general strain after the long patrol without servicing and other problems, was a sure sign that Nasmith had to bring the patrol to an end – but he was not finished yet.

Nasmith set off down the Straits through the first string of mines, searching as he went for a likely target for his last torpedo. He was determined not to return to Moudhros with it but the targets that presented themselves did not merit the expenditure of a 'fish'. It was fast becoming clear that there were to be no pickings further down the Straits so, with a half-crippled boat, an exhausted crew and only one torpedo, he turned about and headed *back up the Straits* in search of more worthy targets. He found one off the Moussa Bank. She was a large transport, lying at anchor, and Nasmith's torpedo sent her to the bottom. Nasmith had used his last torpedo. *Now* was the time to turn for home.

Wheeling round, he set course again down the Straits, fighting as he went against the powerful and fickle cross-currents; then something unusual happened. E-11 suddenly jarred and listed slightly to port. Nasmith puzzled as to what it might be, particularly since he was running quite deep. Then he realized to his horror that the mooring cable of a mine must have become stuck fast in the port hydroplane and E-11 was towing it alongside her. One touch with these deadly horns and it would bring their cruise to an abrupt and fatal end.

Nasmith realized he dared not surface to get it free. The Turkish guns would instantly blast him out of the water. He would have to continue on his way and pray that the flow of water around the submarine's casing would keep the mine away from her. His immediate concern was for his crew and he felt it unwise to add to the tension by telling them of the danger.

There was one other factor in their favour. The mines which infested these waters were of a type designed to blow up surface ships and therefore their horns were built on to the top of the sphere and less likely to come in contact with the submarine. But as they penetrated the last of the minefields in their path and could hear the mooring cables scraping along the side of the boat, Nasmith's fears were heightened when he considered that the mine he was towing might hit another mine or its mooring cable and oblivion might result. For Nasmith that passage through the minefield was nightmarish and it was not until he was clear of the Turkish defences that he allowed his crew to share his secret.

E-11 was now cruising towards Cape Helles, where Nasmith was to rendezvous with the destroyer *Grampus*, but he still had the problem of the mine. He appreciated that if he brought the boat to the surface he would be inviting disaster since the mine would merely float and detonate on the submarine's casing when she reached the surface. To counter this Nasmith trimmed the boat just below the surface and quickly reversed engines. It takes little imagination to appreciate his relief when, with the quick reversal of the boat, the mine's mooring cable slipped free and the mine dropped away into the depths.

The reception given Nasmith and the crew of E-11 was tumultuous. Word of their exploits in the Marmara had spread like wild-fire and now she was back safely. Nasmith's 'bag' for the cruise was one gunboat, two transports, two ammunition ships, two supply ships and another transport driven ashore; but more than this the effect upon Turkish morale was critical. For all these things Nasmith was promoted to commander and awarded the Victoria Cross.

Nasmith and his crew deserved and got a well-earned rest while E-11 was taken to Malta for a complete refit; but even during this lull in action, Nasmith was planning and scheming his return to the Marmara while other submarine commanders were following his example and venturing forth to do battle with the Turks. Boyle was the most prominent of them but he found to his consternation that the Turks had almost completely abandoned the system of shipping their supplies and men across the Marmara and were using the longer but safer rail route around it. This substantially decreased his chances of making big 'kills' and relegated his offensive actions to those against smaller ships plying these waters, most of them carrying contraband.

Nasmith was ready to sally forth into the Marmara only ten days after his return but now his boat had been fitted with a deck gun which would greatly save the unnecessary expenditure of torpedoes when attacking smaller ships. In buoyant mood, Nasmith put to sea once more to return to his favourite haunt. But he, like Boyle and the others, found that the pickings were not quite so rich as they had been and he was involved in many minor actions against smaller ships. He did, however, achieve an ambition when, on the morning of 8 August, he sighted the Turkish battleship *Harridin Barbarossa* which had eluded his torpedoes on two previous occasions. The warship was steaming off Gallipoli on her way to support Turkish defenders repelling Allied landings at Suvla Bay. With her she brought an escorting destroyer but Nasmith found no difficulty in eluding her and sent a torpedo into the battleship which hit her amidships. She began to heel over and turned to beach on the nearby shore but her fate was sealed. The fire that raged within her found the magazine and in a split second she was blown apart and sank.

The remainder of Nasmith's sortie in the Marmara, in concert with Boyle, was a succession of smaller actions since most of the 'big fish' had ceased operating there for fear of submarine attack. Nasmith on more than one occasion tried to disrupt rail traffic by bombarding both stations and lines where they lay close to the shore but the *pièce de resistance* came when D'Oyly Hughes carried out what must have been one of the first 'commando' operations.

There was one weak link in the Turks' railway line at a point where it ran on a viaduct over a deep gorge, and Nasmith reasoned that if the viaduct could be brought down, then the rail link would be severed for some considerable time and the supply of fresh troops and ammunition seriously curtailed for the Turks. Nasmith had already reconnoitred the area and found the viaduct to be built of trellis work, not a very substantial construction which might easily be brought down with the use of his twelve-pounder. He therefore planned just that; greatly against the protests of D'Oyly Hughes, who firmly maintained that it was a job for one man suitably equipped with explosives to get ashore and plant them to blow up the viaduct. However, Nasmith was determined to try the bombardment and one night E-11 crept into the quiet gorge which luckily contained just enough water for her to remain submerged.

At the appointed time, Nasmith brought E-11 to the surface and the guns crew poured on deck and blasted away at the viaduct with shells from the twelve-pounder. For a few minutes there was no reply to the British barrage of fire. Several hits were scored but they achieved little effect. Then suddenly the water around E-11 erupted as Turkish guns positioned around the viaduct opened up at them.

As the submarine's gun seemed to be unable to inflict serious damage on the viaduct, Nasmith ordered the guns crew to stand down and they slid down the conning tower. Hatches were slammed closed and the submarine slipped away out of the gorge. The surface bombardment had failed and once in the open sea and out of range of the Turks' guns, Nasmith and his number one reviewed the situation. There was a broad smile on D'Oyly Hughes' face when Nasmith admitted that it seemed like a job for one man after all and the First Lieutenant immediately claimed the right to undertake the task himself, since he had originated the plan.

A few nights later, Nasmith brought E-11 into the gorge once more and trimmed up so that she lay with only her deck slightly above the water. Moving like phantoms in the night several of the crew slipped on to the casing. Among them was D'Oyly Hughes, his tall well-built figure clad in a swimsuit. A few moments later a small raft was nursed into the water. On it were several bundles wrapped in waterproof coverings and containing the tools of his operation; gun-cotton, a pistol with which to light the fuse, a sharpened bayonet, a whistle and his uniform. His insistence upon taking along his uniform was well-founded for if he were captured it would be proof that he was not a spy and therefore, under the rules of war, could not be legally executed.

After hurried and muted wishes of 'good luck', D'Oyly Hughes edged away from the submarine and struck out for the shore while E-11 slipped beneath the surface, leaving the intrepid 'commando' to his own devices. D'Oyly Hughes' raft nudged up against the shore and he scrambled on to dry land then beached the raft and hid it from view. Then he donned his uniform and, with his packages under his arms, made his way up the steeply sloping hillside until he reached the top. After a cursory glance around to ensure that he had not disturbed the hornets' nest, he stole off into the darkness in search of the railway line.

For a full hour he searched in the inky darkness for the railway line; then he stumbled right into it. Slipping quickly through the night he followed the track until suddenly he stopped dead. In the silent night, he could hear voices ahead of him. Quickly he stowed his explosives at the foot of a tree and crept gingerly forward on all fours, inching his way in the direction of the voices until he found their source – three Turkish sentries sitting talking with their rifles stacked beside them. His progress in that direction was barred so he set off to make a wide detour, scrambling over low walls through farmyards and in and out of a maze of ditches. Then as he slipped through yet another farmyard, the whole world seemed to burst into life around him. He had walked smack into the middle of a chicken run. In an instant chaos reigned as birds fluttered into the air squawking in alarm. D'Oyly Hughes ran as he had never run before and having as he thought put sufficient distance between him and the chickens, dropped behind a wall and lay there panting and breathless. Surely, he thought, that must rouse the sentries; but to his relief no one came searching.

Retracing his steps, but careful not to stumble into the chicken run, he made his way back to the spot where he had secreted his explosives. With the density of sentries guarding the viaduct he realized that blowing it up was out of the question, so he set off to find another spot to lay his charge and found a small culvert which ran through the embankment under the tracks. If he placed his explosives to blow up the culvert the resulting explosion should break the line and take with it the ground supporting it. He packed the explosives in the culvert then levelled his revolver to fire, knowing full well that the resulting report would have Turkish guards closing in on him. He fired and the noise echoed out of the culvert, amplified by its shape, like the roar of a cannon. Already the sentries were leaping out in his direction. But D'Oyly Hughes realized that if they stumbled upon the burning fuse before the five-minute delay had expired they might just be able to defuse it. There was only one course open to him if he was to distract their attention from the explosives.

He leapt on to the track and raced headlong down it *towards* the oncoming sentries. Moments later, he came face to face with them and he raised his revolver, fired two shots then bolted down the embankment towards the shore, amid a hail of bullets from the pursuing Turks. On he charged like a man possessed, and slithered down the slope of the hillside. As he dropped earthwards the low rumble of an explosion reached his ears. He'd done it. The track was, although he could not see it, ripped out from the ground and twisted into a grotesque shape while the culvert was a mere pile of rubble. Repair work would take weeks until the line could be used again and the Turks could ill afford the loss of vital supplies along it.

Reaching the shoreline, D'Oyly Hughes pulled off his shoes and jacket, then leapt into the water. He mustered every ounce of his fast dwindling strength to swim to the safety of the submarine. But as he struggled farther out into the gorge he realized that the submarine was not there waiting for him. He had in fact hit the water some distance away from where he had planned to meet it and he knew that in his condition he would never be able to swim the distance. He turned about, heading back for the shore, and scrambled on to dry land once more, only to hear the Turks crashing through a nearby patch of wood. Hurriedly he picked himself up and ran along the rocky shore until he saw the conning tower of E-11 sticking out of the water. As he plunged into the water and struck out for the submarine Nasmith spotted him and brought the boat in as near as he could to the shore.

Meanwhile the Turks also caught sight of D'Oyly Hughes ploughing through the water and opened up at him sending bullets zipping into the water; but none of them hit the swimmer. From the deck of the submarine, Nasmith's crew returned the fire with rifles until, at last, D'Oyly Hughes' limp and exhausted body was hauled aboard and taken below. With the hatches secure, Nasmith took the boat out to sea once more. Lieutenant D'Oyly Hughes was later awarded the DSO for his night's work.

Nasmith's second patrol ended after twenty-nine days in the Marmara and, even with the restricted operation of enemy ships there, he had to his credit a formidable score of victories which included one battleship, one gunboat, six transports, an armed steamer and *twenty-three* sailing vessels. In addition, he had seriously disrupted the Turkish railway system. To achieve his score he had had to resort to the penetration of enemy harbours and into shallow coastal waters. The Turks were not fools enough to risk their ships in the open sea.

As if his score were not great enough, Nasmith took E-11 back into the Marmara for the longest patrol yet, lasting some forty-seven days, during which he brought havoc to Turkish shipping. He took particular delight in standing off the shore and shelling a locomotive and goods wagons during one of his many raids on the railway lines. After this action, the destroyer *Yar Hissar* was dispatched with all haste to find and destroy E-11 but Nasmith reversed the roles and sent her to the bottom with a well-aimed torpedo.

Nasmith could not resist a return visit to Constantinople harbour, a feat which was becoming a regular occurrence in each of his patrols – no sortie would have been complete without it. He went back again and sent a Turkish steamer to the bottom under their very noses. Following that, a U-boat laid an ambush for Nasmith but it failed and the English commander continued his cruise of destruction.

When he brought the E-11 back through the Straits for the last time he had added to his score of kills eleven steamers, one destroyer and thirty-five sailing vessels.

Nasmith, promoted to captain upon his return to Moudhros, was not to venture into the Marmara again. The Allied troops who had fought so valiantly to secure the peninsula and take Constantinople had failed and the Gallipoli campaign came to an end. No longer was the supremacy of the Marmara of any import and all but a few of the submarines were ordered back to England. Holbrook, Nasmith and Boyle went with them.

Nasmith, dubbed 'The Terror of the Marmara', had chalked up a score unequalled by any of the other commanders who cruised in that inland sea. He had sunk or destroyed one battleship, one destroyer, two gunboats and *eighty-one* other vessels including ammunition ships, supply ships, transports, steamers large and small and fifty-eight sailing vessels, mostly dhows. This staggering total had been achieved in a period of only eight months. He had accounted for more than one-third of the total victories in the Marmara which amounted to some 240 ships sunk.

Nasmith and the other submarine commanders who fought with him in the Marmara unquestionably were responsible for saving countless lives by robbing the Turks of vital supplies during the ill-fated and bloody campaign. How much more horrific the toll of dead would have been on Gallipoli's shores had these gallant commanders and their crews not risked all to do battle in the Marmara.

Home Waters

British submarines operating in North Sea waters did not achieve the startling results their comrades did in the inland seas like the Baltic and the Marmara. Commodore Roger Keyes' Eighth Flotilla was the first to send its boats to war when two of them, E-6 and E-8 – commanded respectively by Lieutenant Commander Talbot and Lieutenant Commander Goodhart – reached their patrol areas in the Heligoland Bight. But their enthusiastic commanders, bent on getting quickly into action, were in for a taste of the utter boredom which was to accompany these early patrols.

For six days and nights both boats carried out patrols but neither one of them was fortunate enough to get into action before returning to base. This, alas, was to be the general pattern for almost all the patrols and little or no offensive success was achieved, although there were moments of excitement. These isolated incidents invariably occurred when a submarine commander was preparing to launch an attack and found himself on the point of being rammed by an escorting destroyer. Inexperience in actual battle conditions was the prime cause of these misadventures.

During the ferrying of the British Expeditionary Force across the English Channel, B-, C- and E-class submarines took on a defensive role, standing guard over the ships and acting as close support vessels for the giant transport ships. Then with the massive sea-borne transportation completed, the Eighth Flotilla returned to its patrol duties; but in the main commanders and crew alike found themselves faced with the task of relieving the tedium of these patrols.

During one of his patrols, Lieutenant Commander Leir, in E-4, surfaced to find himself amid a German fishing fleet and found a novel way of replenishing his boat's depleted food store. He drew alongside a few of the boats and threatened to torpedo them if they did not hand over a supply of fish. The non-combatant fisherman saw this as a blatant act of piracy and hastily signalled for assistance. In due course two German naval trawlers put out from their base to deal with the 'buccaneer' and the first on the scene got his just deserts when the boat was ripped apart by one of Leir's torpedoes. His companion, sensing that he might suffer a similar fate, discreetly departed from the scene with as much alacrity as he could muster.

Leir picked up the trawler's survivors and furnished them with a lifeboat which he proceeded to tow to a German light-ship, several miles off. Before putting them on board it, he picked four of them as prisoners and they duly spent the re-mainder of the war in an English p.o.w. camp. This incident did much to lighten an otherwise tedious patrol.

In the Heligoland Bight there were brief flurries of activity, mainly between German destroyers and the occasional larger ship. British submarines launched attacks on them but more often than not they ended in failure for two primary reasons: either their quarry was steering a fast zig-zag course, making a difficult target or, having fired a torpedo, it would for no explic-able reason run deep beneath the target or veer off course. This idiosyncrasy inherent in the British torpedo did, as we have already seen, rob commanders of many worthy targets.

There was one noteworthy difference between submarine operations in these waters and those of the Baltic and the Marmara. For the first time and consistently afterwards, British submarines found themselves duelling with German U-boats. In one early encounter, Lieutenant Commander Leir narrowly missed bagging two U-boats when, on 10 September 1914, he sighted U-23 cruising on the surface off Heligoland and, run-ning at periscope depth, he pursued her until he had manoeuvred into firing position. Alas, his torpedo swept under-neath the German boat and was spotted. But then sweeping the sea with his periscope Leir sighted another U-boat. No sooner had he done so than the U-boat's deck gun erupted and shells began plopping into the water around E-4. Without hesitation, Leir loosed off another torpedo in a 'snap' shot at the second German but his aim was not true and it too missed. The sight of the torpedo streaking through the water towards him sent the German commander scurrying away and the other boat did likewise. It was an ineffective encounter but not all of them were to be so.

Max Horton was the first to spill blood in a major way with the sinking of the German cruiser *Hela*; quickly followed four days later by a German destroyer. For the German Navy 13 September was an unlucky day but it was an equally unlucky one for the British Submarine Service. It was on that day that she suffered her first loss when the Royal Australian Navy's submarine AE-1, an identical twin of Horton's E-9, was lost with all hands in the Bismarck Sea. What caused her loss no one knows.

In spite of its overwhelming power, the Royal Navy fared badly in the war at sea. The expected early victory by the British Fleet over the German Fleet had not come and enemy submarines were meeting with considerable success against British warships. *Pathfinder, Aboukir, Hogue* and *Cressy* were all sunk by U-boats and a feeling of unease was spreading throughout the country which sorely needed a morale boost. The retrogressive situation was not helped when the British submarine E-3 was torpedoed and sunk by the German U-27 while on patrol off the mouth of the River Ems.

The potency of the German submarines did not go unnoticed by Churchill who, when the ageing veteran Admiral Lord Fisher was called out of retirement to take over as First Sea Lord, sent a memorandum instructing him to '... propose without delay the largest possible programme of submarine building to be delivered in from twelve to twenty-four months from the present time'.

Fisher got the programme under way but he went to the United States to have his ships built in a bid to avoid overburdening the already stretched British yards. At that time the United States was neutral and this posed the problem that, by supplying ships to the British Navy, she would affect her neutrality. Fisher overcame this by having them built without armament, with the intention of taking them to Canada to have them fitted out after completion. Alas, his scheme went awry, for the United States ultimately refused to release them and it was 1917 before they finally arrived.

Disaster was to strike the Submarine Service again very soon for, on 3 November 1915, three German battle-cruisers closed in on the English fishing port of Yarmouth and began a bombardment. As it happened, there were submarines D-5 (Lieutenant Commander Godfrey Herbert) and E-10 (Lieutenant Commander Fraser) tied up in harbour at Yarmouth and their commanders took them out to do what they could to halt the bombardment. On the way out, D-5, in the van of the chase, struck a mine, and sank almost immediately, leaving only those officers and men who had been on the bridge, in the water. Only three of them survived, among them Godfrey Herbert.

More tragedy was looming close for the British Submarine Service when three weeks later another D-class submarine, the D-2, was cruising in heavy seas. Her commander was swept overboard and lost. The submarine returned to port but left for another patrol the following day and vanished without trace.

Submariners in those early days of war were masters of the art of invention. They had to be for their seemingly routine patrols were punctuated by engine failures and all sorts of mechanical troubles. One of the finest examples of improvisation was enacted aboard the Laurenti-designed British submarine S-1 when she was on patrol off Horn Reef with Lieutenant Commander Kellet as her captain. The patrol had passed without incident, an unusual feature, for S-1 had suffered more than her fair share of engine trouble from her 650 hp diesel engines. Then trouble hit her like a thunderbolt when her engines faltered and came to a stop. Kellet asked for a report from the engineer officer whose glum expression forewarned him of the worst. The main bearings had gone and this was no minor problem. Repairs could be effected only in port and that was a good 300 miles away; too far for her to reach on electric power.

The situation seemed without solution. They had no way of calling for help since their wireless had a range of only forty miles and there was little likelihood of a friendly vessel passing their way. Kellet had almost resigned himself to scuttling the boat, when an enemy vessel came along, and being taken prisoner. It was then that the germ of an idea occurred to him. He ordered the submarine dived under battery power and took her down to thirty feet, then when a thorough check had been made that everything was in working order, he took her right down to the sea-bed where she lay for the remainder of the day.

When night came, Kellet took S-1 to periscope depth. In the half darkness he saw what he had been looking for – a German fishing boat innocently going about her business. A boarding party got ready, armed with rifles, revolvers and cutlasses while Kellet brought S-1 up to the surface alongside the fishing boat. The fishermen on board were riveted to the spot when the submarine gushed up from the depths like a whale, shedding water from her upper casing as she emerged. The conning tower hatch was thrown open and the boarding party swarmed out and leapt the gap between the two vessels. Adopting the fiercest postures they could muster, the boarding party brandished cutlasses and waved muzzles in the faces of the terrified crew. It was a bloodless capture for no resistance was offered and the petrified Germans willingly obeyed the clipped orders to go aboard the submarine.

In the meantime, two of the submarine's ERAs (Engine Room Artificers) who had had some experience with coal-fired boilers went below and, with a tow rope firmly secured to the submarine, the fishing vessel began towing the submarine the 300 miles back to base at Harwich. Meanwhile the fishermen, still unable to believe what had become of them, were looked after by the submarine's crew. By some fluke of good fortune, S-1 was not spotted by German patrols and, after a cruise dogged by repeated breakdowns, she arrived at Harwich where the fishermen were duly dispatched for internment and the crew of S-1 to a well-earned celebration.

The refusal of the German High Seas Fleet to come out into the open and do battle with the Grand Fleet denied the British submarines operating in the North Sea the opportunity of carrying out any major offensive operations. U-boats were having an unqualified success in the North Sea and against merchant shipping in general. 1915 saw them patrolling close to British fleet anchorages and sinking major units as they came out, either on patrol or exercise. Furthermore they were indulging in some particularly nasty acts of barbarism against fishing trawlers which they sank piecemeal. These very acts were to prove the undoing of more than one U-boat commander, for a cunning ruse was devised to counter them.

It was Acting Paymaster Spickernell, on Admiral Beatty's staff, who sparked off the idea of using the trawlers as decoys to lure the U-boats. The plan was simplicity itself. An armed trawler would purposely go about its business in heavily U-boat infested waters, intentionally presenting itself as an easy target for the hungry German commanders; but they would be in for a shock when they set themselves up for an attack. Submerged and attached to the trawler by a tow line together with a telephone link would be a C-class submarine. The trawler crew, having spotted the U-boat, would play out a scene of panic and make to abandon ship while one of them informed the British submarine commander of the U-boat's position. The British commander would then drop the tow and launch his attack on the U-boat. The first successful attack launched in this manner proved rather more dangerous than had been anticipated.

On the morning of 23 June 1915, the trawler *Taranaki* was playing the role of 'lure' for the big German fish, with the submarine C-24 in tow when U-40 was spotted stalking her about 1,000 yards astern. Her captain immediately rang the C-24's commander, Lieutenant Taylor, and warned him of the German's presence. At once the trawler's crew enacted the scene of drama on her deck with the 'panic crew' hastily taking to a lifeboat. The U-boat was setting herself up for the classic surface attack. The trawler, in the German's opinion, did not merit a torpedo and she closed to shell her.

But meanwhile, things were not going well for the British submarine. The thick tow line refused to part company with it and this posed a serious problem for if the Germans succeeded in sinking the trawler it would haul the submarine to the bottom with it. There was only one thing for it. The 'panic crew' would have to release the tow from their end and hope the Germans did not see them doing it and suspect that all was not what it seemed. This was quickly done, luckily without the Germans tumbling to what was happening; but it brought with it a moment of tension for the C-24's crew. The heavy weight of the hawser upset the trim of the boat and the submarine nosed towards the sea-bed. It was only by the skill of the First Lieutenant that she caught her trim again and manoeuvred in to attack.

By now the first of U-40's shells was lancing through the air and landing close to the *Taranaki*, but as the gun continued to roar Taylor released his torpedo. The U-boat was a sitting duck and it hit her square amidships, ripping her open and casting its only survivors into the sea before plunging to the depths. C-24 and the trawler returned to their base, confident that the new ruse was still a secret.

The following month, a similar action took place when U-23 was sent to the bottom by C-27, near the entrance to Fair Island Channel; but alas, the success of the trawler decoy system was short-lived. In August two losses occurred within a short space of each other. C-33, making for base with the trawler *Malta*, ran into a British minefield, struck a mine and was sunk with all hands. Only three weeks later C-29 fell to a similar fate when she too hit a mine near the estuary of the Humber and her entire complement was lost. These losses, coupled with the knowledge that the Germans were now aware of the trawler decoys, brought an end to this form of operation.

For British submarines, the saga of their exploits in the North Sea and its immediate environs was one of a succession of opportunities missed and plain bad luck. A classic example of this came in April 1916 when Admiral Scheer brought a squadron of German battle-cruisers for another bombardment of Yarmouth and Lowestoft. No fewer than eleven British submarines raced to intercept the powerful German ships, but not one of them managed to get in a shot. Then during Scheer's return to Germany E-22, patrolling in the North Sea in the hope of snatching a shot when Scheer's squadron passed, was sunk by UB-18.

But not all the British submarines met with such misfortune. In May of that same year, an incident occurred which must be quite unique in the annals of submarine warfare.

British submarines operating in the Heligoland Bight had been dogged by interference by German Zeppelins. The airships patrolling that area constantly threatened the submarines with their bombs and many narrow escapes were suffered. Then on 4 May, during a minelaying operation in the Borkum area and near the Vyl Light Vessel, the German airship L.7 was slightly crippled by the guns of the British ships *Galatea* and *Phaeton*. She immediately began to lose height and wheeled round to head back for her base at Tondern. On her way she was sighted by the British submarine E-31 captained by Lieutenant Commander Fielman. Fearing that he might be attacked, for the Zeppelin was close overhead, Fielman dived; but when no bombs came he brought E-31 back up to the surface and found the great cigar-shaped Zeppelin had lost height, and far from wishing to attack the submarine seemed to be fighting for her own life by struggling back to base. The opportunity was just too good to miss and Fielman ordered the gun crew to close up. By then the Zeppelin was almost in the water.

Within a couple of minutes high explosive shells from E-31's deck gun were bursting into the side of the Zeppelin and the first flicker of flames could be seen emanating from the gas-filled silver hulk. Soon, as more shells were pumped into her, the flames spread and her crew began to leap out of the gondola slung beneath her almost 100 feet into the water. Slowly, almost majestically, the now flaming ball of fire dipped and hit the water, casting up a towering mountain of steam.

With German surface ships in the area racing in to come to the aid of the airship's survivors, Fielman and his crew had little time to ponder upon their handiwork and slipped away from the scene, amply rewarded for their day's work. Hard on the heels of this epic action came the Battle of Jutland, the clash of giants in which both the British and German Fleets claimed to have won the day. But no submarines took part in the actions.

War patrols continued in the Bight and Skagerrak but they were tedious affairs. This frustration is perhaps highlighted by an incident involving Lieutenant Varley of H-5. In July 1916 he was ordered to patrol in the Heligoland Bight off Terschelling but he found that, as so many times before, there was nothing doing there. Downright frustration can drive a man to do things he normally wouldn't, and this is what happened to Varley. He just couldn't see the sense of patrolling an area where there were no ships to be found so he committed what his Lords and Masters regarded as one of the cardinal sins – he left his patrol area contrary to orders and went off hunting on his own. Varley must have realized only too well what the ultimate penalty would be, but both he and his crew had reached a stage where they were prepared to risk the consequences.

Varley set course for Borkum where he hoped he'd find juicy pickings and bag a few ships, and in so doing prove the misguidedness of his superiors or at least lessen his misdemeanour in leaving his patrol area. But to his disgust he found the cupboard bare of targets. He was now, metaphorically, in deep water. If he didn't find a worthy target and send it to the bottom, he would be risking a court martial. But when it seemed that his fate was sealed an opportunity presented itself as a flotilla of destroyers hove into sight. Varley attacked but the enemy was travelling at such speed and weaving such a zig-zag course that his torpedoes missed their mark and were lost. The proverbial 'goose' had, it seemed, been 'done to a turn'.

Not only had he wasted torpedoes in a hopeless attack but his periscope had developed a fault and could not be fully withdrawn; a factor which would make future attacks very difficult. To add further to the miseries, H-5 had lost a valuable tool kit while carrying out repairs on the surface. In her anxiety to dive quickly when an enemy attack seemed imminent, the tools had been left on the deck and were gone for ever.

Varley's misfortune could not last for ever, he reasoned; and as luck would have it, he was proved right. The German U-51 slipped out of her base to take up a patrol in the Atlantic and as she proceeded along the surface she cruised right into Varley's sights. A single torpedo shot towards her and ripped her apart. Joyous at his success, Varley surfaced, bent on grabbing some prisoners or at least some evidence of his success to show his superiors upon his return. But his conning tower had hardly emerged from the water when the order to crash-dive came from Varley's lips. German patrol vessels were racing in on him and depth charge crews were closing for an attack.

H-5 went deep and as she plunged downward she was knocked about by the fierce detonations of the depth charges as they tumbled into the sea. This underwater bombardment ultimately ceased and no damage was done to H-5, but the Germans were far from finished for they then began a series of wire-sweeps during which the submarine almost came to grief. The enemy destroyers were combing the water for H-5 but Varley's luck held and he succeeded in slipping clear.

In spite of his success, he had no proof of it and the wrath of his flotilla captain descended upon him. He and he alone was responsible for breaking the rules and the onus lay squarely upon his shoulders. The tongue-lashing the young Canadian commander received from the flotilla captain was fierce but luckily for him his chief was himself a seasoned submariner and appreciated his subordinate's situation and the temptations to which he had been subjected. In his report to the Admiralty, the captain did not defend Varley's breaking the rules but he did praise his skill as a commander and his tenacity in pressing home an attack on a U-boat. After a suitable period elapsed, during which Varley was given time to reflect upon his wrongdoing, he was admitted to the Distinguished Service Order for his gallantry!

The North Sea never did match the Baltic and Marmara as a 'happy hunting ground' for British submarines. Targets were few and boredom a constant companion on patrols.

But if this prospect were not bleak enough, events in Home Waters were marred by what was unquestionably the blackest hour in the history of the British Submarine Service – the introduction of the K-class steam-powered boats. If ever there was an ill-conceived and badly designed boat, this was it. The advent of this submarine was the spark that lit the fire of disaster.

The C-in-C Grand Fleet, misguidedly believing that the German Navy possessed fleet submarines, pressed for the introduction of a similar type to operate with his own fleet. At that time the diesel engines in use in British submarines were incapable of producing sufficient power to enable them to operate in this role and achieve a high enough surface speed to keep up with the fleet. But steam engines, it was found, could produce the required twenty-one knots and more. So it was that the K-class steam-driven submarine was introduced. It was a giant alongside all the others with a submerged displacement of 2,565 tons and a length of 338 feet. It could produce a surface speed of twenty-four knots; more than adequate to keep up with the fleet. But that was where its advantages stopped. The K-class submarine dived on steam power at about twenty knots and being so long, the bows reached a dangerous depth while the stern was still on the surface. In addition, it was difficult to handle, both on the surface and while submerged.

From the very beginning, the K-class boats launched a trail of disaster. In all, some twenty-seven units were ordered. They were numbered K-1 to K-21 and K-23 to K-28. Within a short time of its completion, K-13 sank during trials. She was salvaged and renumbered K-22. The development of these boats continued long after the war had ended. Of the boats completed, six were lost, *all in accidents*, five were cancelled, four were converted into submarine monitors while building was in progress and those that remained were eventually scrapped. In the accidents, they suffered a fearful loss of life – all for nothing. As one submarine commander of the time commented, 'The only good thing about "K" boats was that they never engaged the enemy.' Submariners hated them.

While the tragedy of the K boats was being enacted, the submariners in other submarine types were finding precious little to boost their morale and they too were suffering severe setbacks. In January 1918 no fewer than five boats were lost in what was the darkest month of the war for the Submarine Service. The trail of disaster and near-disaster continued and was made all the more heart-rending when on more than one occasion British submarines came under attack from their own surface vessels due to mistaken identity. One, the D-3, was mistakenly identified as a U-boat by the crew of a French airship and bombed to destruction.

In April 1918 the submariners got a shot in the arm to buoy-up their morale. Late in that month Admiral Scheer brought his High Seas Fleet out from its base to attack the British Scandinavian convoys, and while steaming towards the area the battle-cruiser *Moltke* suffered mechanical trouble. She was taken in tow by the *Oldenberg* and the two ships headed back for port. As they did so Lieutenant Allen in E-42 was lying in wait and fired four torpedoes, one which hit the limping *Moltke*. She sustained only minor damage as a result of Allen's 'sting' and was able to reach harbour, but the whole episode ended ignominiously for the High Seas Fleet.

In spite of the reduced effectiveness of the German U-boat against British supply ships – because of the advent of more sophisticated anti-submarine devices and stronger surface patrols – the German submarines were still a thorn in their side and Roger Keyes, by then a Rear-Admiral, gave birth to the idea of bottling them up in their bases in Belgium. Thus came about the famous Zeebrugge raid.

Part of the raid called for the use of two submarines which were to carry out a 'suicide' mission in order to destroy the viaduct which linked the Zeebrugge Mole to the mainland. The plan was that a submarine, packed with tons of explosives, would scuttle beneath the viaduct and blow up, hopefully bringing the viaduct down in the process. In a bid to guard against accidents, a back-up submarine would accompany the one which was to 'make the hit'.

The submarines chosen for the task were of the old C-class boats of the Sixth Flotilla based at Portsmouth. They were C-1 under the command of Lieutenant Newbold and C-3 under the command of Lieutenant Sandford. Lieutenant Commander Francis Sandford, a brother of the submarine captain, was to accompany the two submarines on their mission in a picket boat and act as over-all commander of the attack.

The scheme was that the picket boat would retrieve the submarine crews after they had set their explosive charges; but even so it was fully appreciated by all who took part that their chances of returning were decidedly slim, and because of this the minimum number of crewmen were to take part.

At the appointed time the submarines, in company with their picket boat, were towed to their slip-off points and they parted with their parent ships and nosed in through the darkness towards their targets. But as they did so they lost contact with each other and Sandford in C-3 found himself alone and closing the viaduct. On the bridge, a smoke canister was brought into operation to screen their approach but a strong wind blew the veiling smoke in the wrong direction. A few moments later a flare arched into the night sky and illuminated the scene. Almost instantly, searchlights positioned on the mole were switched on and they coned the submarine; but for some inexplicable reason the gunners on the heavily defended mole did not fire. They must have assumed that Sandford's submarine was a U-boat.

The minutes ticked tensely by until with a grinding crash C-3 rammed the supporting trellis-work of the viaduct. Sandford lost no time in lighting the fuses on the five tons of amatol explosive while the others released the motor boat which they were to use for their escape bid. With the fuse burning away the six men of the crew leapt into the boat; but to their horror they found the engine was malfunctioning and had to use the oars. No sooner had they come out from the shelter of the viaduct than the Germans tumbled to their intentions and a hail of machine-gun fire lashed the boat. In the first burst Stoker Bindall was hit, and as Sandford tried to go to his aid he too was hit in the hand. Two of the others, Roxburgh and Harner, rowed with all their might to put some distance between them and the German gunners but the swift-flowing tide persistently drove them back from whence they had come.

Again the gunners found their mark and Petty Officer Harner was riddled with bullets. Cleaver, one of the other crewmen, shoved the inert figure out of the way and bent his back to the oars but, as he moved, Sandford at the tiller received another hit, this time in the thigh. He could no longer steer the boat and Lieutenant Howell-Price took over from him. Sandford sat in the well of the boat amid a pool of blood seeping from wounds, and urged his men on. But then heavier guns opened up at them and pom-pom shells rained into the water. In spite of the intensity of the fire the two oarsmen rowed with all their might while Howell-Price, oblivious of the torrent of fire, steered the boat.

Mercifully, the fuse burning in the submarine at last reached the explosives and C-3 all but disappeared in a great ball of fire, taking a great chunk of the viaduct with her – including the guns which had put up such a murderous torrent of fire at the tiny boat-load of men.

Sandford and the others searched around before finding C-1, which had not reached the viaduct, and were taken aboard. For his part in that operation, Sandford was awarded the Submarine Service's fourth and last Victoria Cross of the war.

Following the Zeebrugge raid, patrolling British submarines had a brief but successful burst of good fortune for, in a comparatively short space of time, four U-boats and a destroyer were sent to the bottom. But this run of success was short-lived and in the dying months of the war, before the Armistice, the Navy lost more submarines than it reaped rewards.

The submarine campaign fought in the North Sea waters had not been a glorious campaign like that of the Marmara or the Baltic, but the same courage and determination permeated the crews of the submarines, a core of valour which was to be exemplified two decades later, when Britain's submariners were called again to war in the deep.

2

British Submarines in The Second World War

By sheer coincidence the Royal Navy had exactly the same number of operational submarines at the outset of the Second World War as did its opposite number the *Kriegsmarine* – fifty-seven. Essentially, that is where the similarity ended. The tactics evolved for the use of British submarines were substantially different from those envisaged for the units of the U-boat arm. As in the First World War, Germany had a numerically inferior surface fleet to that of the Royal Navy. It followed, therefore, that she was unlikely to risk her fleet in open conflict with the British Fleet, and in adopting such an attitude she denied the Royal Navy's submarines the opportunity of catching the 'big fish'. Because of its geographical position, Germany had no need to send her surface fleet to sea in the role of 'protector' for supply convoys. The victuals which fed the Nazi war machine could be transported to the Reich via landlocked seas like the Baltic or down the seas of coastal Norway, screened from view or attack by a thousand islands. The German Merchant Marine was not to suffer the devastating losses inflicted upon its British counterpart; they had no vast ocean to cross for their vital supplies. British submarine successes against merchantmen were to be tiny by comparison with the U-boats; except that is, in areas other than Home Waters. The opportunities of inflicting such enormous damage and achieving vast personal scores were not to come to the British submarine commander the way they did to the U-boat captain.

In the initial stages of the war, because of the seas being empty of enemy ships, boredom set in for the crews of British submarines. Day after day, night after night, patrolling the same line at periscope depth throughout the day and on the surface at night, stationed off the enemy coast waiting, watching for the tell-tale hint that would herald the departure of the German Fleet which did not come. With monotonous invariability, submarine commanders returned to base with a full load of torpedoes and a crew bored and lethargic through soul-destroying repetition of the same tasks which they carried out as second nature in any case. Life aboard the British submarines was dull and routine but 'moments of intense fright' did come, and when they did the British submariner rose to the occasion with skill and determination. The enthusiasm which had been suppressed into latency by days of inactivity, uncovered itself and rose to a crest. One of those fortunate enough to enjoy more than one fleeting moment of action and a break from the tiring monotony of uneventful patrol was Lieutenant Commander Edward Bickford, captain of HMS/M *Salmon*, one of the 700-ton S-class submarines of the Harwich Flotilla.

Bickford and *Salmon* were recalled from duty with the Mediterranean fleet immediately upon the opening of hostilities with Germany, but as he brought his boat into the familiar waters of the English Channel he got a brief and almost mortal taste of combat when *Salmon* and other boats of his flotilla came under attack from *British* anti-submarine patrol vessels. The Royal Navy had not wasted its time in the development of anti-submarine warfare in the pause between the wars and had reached a new peak of efficiency, as Bickford quickly found out. Happily, the flashing of recognition signals brought the attack to a halt and the submarines escaped unscathed, but the action had very nearly resulted in a lethal conclusion.

Salmon had no sooner reached her new Harwich base than she was turned about and assigned a patrol station off the enemy's coast. December saw her on station at the mouth of the Skagerrak, standing guard over that stretch of sea which led into and out of the Baltic, in the hope of catching German shipping passing through. Bickford and the crew of *Salmon* underwent the same grinding routine, scouring the empty seas in search of fodder for his torpedoes, but the sea remained wintry and desolate. It appeared that this was just to be another routine patrol.

Darkness gave way to the half-light of dawn on 4 December 1939 just as it had done on previous days, and revealing again an empty sea bereft of enemy ships. The coming of dawn was the signal for *Salmon* to seek invisibility beneath the waves, to take up her watch through the periscope's eye. Bickford, worn out after a long and tiring night on watch, fell exhausted into his bunk while Lieutenant Wykeham-Martyn resumed the watch at the periscope. *Salmon*'s captain had not been asleep long when the call came for him to go to the control room. There he found his First Lieutenant intently peering through the periscope, fixed on an object in the sea. Bickford glanced into the periscope's lens. Steering on the surface on a northerly course was a German submarine, U-36. The enemy boat presented a far from ideal target. *Salmon*'s Asdic had already caught the enemy in its beam and was holding it while Bickford negotiated the boat into a firing position, 5,000 yards from the German. He was taking no chances and fired a salvo of six torpedoes which shot out of the bow tubes and streaked through the murky sea towards their goal.

Then came the anxious minutes of waiting. Had Bickford correctly computed the range, course and bearing? Was the deflection angle right to bring the torpedoes into collision with their target? It was to be more than four minutes before the answer was known and Bickford brought the periscope up and fixed the lens on the enemy boat. A split second later the water around the U-boat erupted in a turmoil as a torpedo slammed into her and blasted her into pieces. The sea gushed into the air as it was cast skyward by the blast. Bickford watched awestruck as the sea subsided, leaving only fragmented wreckage strewn about it. The U-boat was nowhere to be seen. She and her crew had met their fate.

Bickford and *Salmon*'s crew, joyous at their success, had a long wait before fresh pickings came their way but the incident that occurred on 12 December served to illustrate one of the difficulties under which British submarine commanders had to conduct their war with the imposition of strict adherence to the rules. Cruising at periscope depth that morning, Bickford caught sight of the 51,700-ton German Atlantic liner *Bremen*, the pride of her passenger fleet. The German liner presented a beautiful and tempting target, cruising only a mile from *Salmon*'s position; but to claim her, Bickford had first to bring her to and have a boarding party examine her to determine whether or not she was a legitimate prize of war. If so, then a prize crew would be put aboard and take her to an Allied port. The loss of such a sizeable ship would, Bickford knew, prove a considerable dent in the strength of the German merchant marine.

Bickford surfaced and signalled the liner to stop but *Salmon*'s signals were ignored and Bickford was on the point of loading his deck gun to fire a shot across her bows when a German aircraft swept over the sea and forced him to seek succour in the depths. The temptation to unleash a salvo of torpedoes into the liner was great but Bickford had to exercise restraint. Unlike the German U-boat commander Lemp, Bickford wanted no part in another *Athenia* affair. Somewhat disappointed at not netting such a valuable catch, he resumed his patrol but the very next day brought him the chance he had been waiting for when he saw three light cruisers, the *Leipzig*, *Nürnberg* and *Koln* and a group of escorting destroyers.

This powerful force of warships was homeward bound from a sortie off the English coast. They were some six miles off and Bickford ordered full speed to manoeuvre into a firing position, his eyes intent on the cruisers. What a prize to sink just one of them; but his hopes of achieving such a victory were quickly dashed for the warships' superior surface speed took them well outside the range of Bickford's torpedoes. But just as it seemed that he was to suffer yet another disappointment the three light cruisers altered course and steered towards *Salmon*. Hopes rose again and the submarine was a flurry of activity as the torpedomen closed up. Six torpedoes were fired at the cruisers from 5,000 yards; three of them found their targets – two hit *Leipzig* and one slammed into the *Nürnberg*. Immediately, Bickford took *Salmon* deep while the escorting destroyers swept the area in search of her, dropping dozens of depth charges. For five hours the German destroyers relentlessly scoured the sea for *Salmon* but they were not up to it and at last broke off their search.

When Bickford finally came to the surface the ships were gone. However, the cruisers had not sunk, although both of them had been severely damaged, and they limped back to their base. Bickford need not have been disappointed at not sinking them for the damage inflicted was so severe that *Nürnberg* was out of action for five months while *Leipzig* never again saw action. The Germans were to get their revenge six months later, however, when in June 1940, Bickford took *Salmon* on patrol and was never seen again. She was lost with all hands; in all probability to a German mine.

9 January 1940 brought with it the vital shot in the arm the Submarine Service so desperately needed when Vice-Admiral Sir Max Horton was appointed to command the submarines. Horton, the hero of the Baltic campaign of the First World War, was a popular figure among submariners, greatly respected by all as a man and as a brilliant submariner. He had lost none of his flair for action during the years between the wars and it was with a feeling of renewed optimism among the men of the Silent Service that Horton took up his new post.

Alas, Horton's new command was almost instantly marred by tragedy when, on the three successive days following his appointment, three British submarines were lost as a result of enemy action; the first to be lost in this way in the war. However tragic these losses were, there were happier days not far off. Horton reviewed his submarine commanders. He quickly realized that many of his commanders were too old for the job. He remembered the intense strain he had suffered as a submarine captain during the previous war. He replaced the older men with young officers, buoyant with energy and enthusiasm and infinitely more able to withstand prolonged stress in combat situations.

Throughout the earlier months of the war, the submarine commanders had had their hands shackled by International Law, which as we have seen imposed strict rules upon them regarding what they could and could not sink. Germany was using the 'fair play' methods adhered to by the British to her advantage; moving the vital iron ore as well as troops in merchant ships sailing under neutral flags. This crafty piece of subterfuge was uncovered when Commander Phillips in the U-class submarine *Ursula* brought the SS *Heddernheim* to a halt. Her captain protested that she was Esthonian but Phillips wasn't having any of it and when the merchantman tried to sail off, *Ursula*'s deck gun brought her to a stop and the crew abandoned ship. When the crew was safely in the boats, Phillips sank the *Hedderheim* with a torpedo after he had discovered that not only was her crew German but they had been carrying 7,000 tons of iron ore. The Germans, under the guise of innocent neutral merchant ships, continued their clandestine activities. The British submarine commanders knew their game but were denied the chance of scoring victories by their strict adherence to these international rules. The time was not far off, however, when the submarines in the North Sea were to have a free hand and the Service was to enjoy a 'happy time'.

Horton found his force of submarines growing in strength with fourteen French submarines coming under his wing. This coupled with the commissioning of new British submarines gave him a potent force with which to wage war and he was soon to need every one of them.

Spring brought with it the threat of a German invasion of Norway. Hitler desperately wanted to secure the Norwegian ports to enable his supply vessels carrying war materials down the coast to do so with greater impunity. Horton got wind of the intended invasion and towards the end of March guessed that it was bound to come soon. He marshalled his forces and sent nineteen submarines to sea to back up those already operating off the Norwegian coast and standing sentinel over the possible exit points of the German invasion fleet. Horton's move was a gamble of inordinate proportions simply because if the invasion did not come within the first half of April, then almost his entire fleet would be obliged to return to base for refuelling, and this would leave the invasion waters unguarded and the German invasion fleet free to launch its attack on Norway without hindrance. But Horton's intuition was well-founded and the move paid off.

The first confirmation that Horton's prediction had come true came on the morning of 7 April when intelligence reports confirmed that the assault was about to be launched. The following day it began, with streams of transport ships supported by warships heading to invade both Norway and Denmark. At mid-day, the Polish submarine *Orzel*, operating under Horton's command, sighted and sank the transport *Rio de Janeiro*, close to Christiansund South. On board her were many German troops. Then only an hour later, Commander Seale, in the submarine *Trident*, sent the tanker *Poseidonia* to the bottom. But these were to be the only major pickings of the day. No other contacts were made.

The following morning, 9 April, the invasions began; but the vast majority of the invasion forces reached their destinations unharmed, having squirmed through the net of British submarines. Although, from the German point of view, that part of the operation had gone more or less according to plan and their assault troops had been landed, their ships were still vulnerable since they had yet to make their way back to their home bases in Germany and it was while they were doing this that the Silent Service enjoyed its heyday.

There was one over-riding factor which was crucial to the submarine effort and that was the lifting of restrictions on sinking on sight. Without *carte blanche* from the Admiralty there would be little hope of achieving any significant victories over the enemy. Horton implored the Admiralty to give their consent and on 9 April in the early evening, signals were dispatched giving the submarine commanders the 'green light' to sink *any* ship sighted within ten miles of the Norwegian coast. This was the opportunity the British commanders had been waiting for. Lieutenant Commander Hutchison, commanding the 1,100-ton Triton class submarine *Truant* was the first to notch up a victory that day. Throughout that day, *Truant* had been hounded by anti-submarine craft and had had the nerve-racking task of dodging them as they scoured the sea for British submarines. Every time Hutchison ventured a look through the periscope, he had to dive for safety as a patrolling German boat turned his way. This frustrating situation lasted all day until the evening when the anti-submarine craft changed their area of operation and left *Truant* in peace. At last Hutchison was able to make a full sweep of the sea and when he sighted an object on the horizon he quickly realized that all the frustrations and danger of the day had been worth it. Ploughing through the waves towards *Truant* was the German cruiser *Karlsruhe* with three attendant torpedo boats. The small formation of ships was weaving a zig-zag course which made the target all the more difficult for Hutchison; and as luck would have it, they changed course when the full salvo of torpedoes shot out of *Truant*'s tubes.

The torpedoes streaked through the sea and were spotted on board *Karlsruhe*. She swerved out of the way but she was not fast enough and one of them caught her aft, shattering her steering gear and stopping her engines. Tons of water poured into the German cruiser and she began to sink while her crew abandoned ship. She was mortally wounded and taking in water fast. With the crew safely off the ship, one of the torpedo boats finished off the job with two torpedoes.

Radios aboard the German ships were abuzz with the warning of a British submarine in the area and, before *Truant* could make good her escape, the anti-submarine boats which had hunted her all day returned, bent on destroying her. For *nineteen* hours they kept up an almost constant attack on the submarine during which she was depth charged. Leaks developed in her casing, the air became foul as the hours passed and breathing became increasingly difficult for the crew. At last, on the point of total collapse through oxygen starvation, Hutchison brought the boat to periscope depth and risked a look. To his relief he found the sea empty of the enemy and mercifully he was able to surface and the cool, refreshing air swept into the boat. Hutchison set course for home, while the engineers went about repairing the damage which, by some miracle of wizardry on the part of the crew, was accomplished before they reached base.

That same day, the *Sunfish* accounted for the 7,000-ton merchantman *Amasis* but it was the following day that the scores began to soar. *Sunfish* scored another victory, sinking the 2,500-ton merchant ship *Antares*; but the most notable successes of the day came from *Triton*, under Lieutenant Commander Pizey, and *Spearfish*, Lieutenant Commander Forbes. In the late afternoon, Pizey sighted a convoy of transports under destroyer escort. With consummate skill he slipped under the defensive destroyer screen and shot a salvo of six torpedoes, and three of them found their targets. Two torpedoes sank the transports *Friedenau* and *Wigbert* while another caught the patrol vessel *Rau.6* amidships and blasted her clear out of the water. Forbes's success was worthy since one of the transports was laden with 900 troops as well as vital supplies.

The German escorts immediately began a concerted attack upon *Triton* and they might well have succeeded in claiming the boat which had sunk their transports had it not been for the appearance of the *Spearfish* nearby, which diverted the attentions of the anti-submarine vessels and allowed Pizey to slip away unscathed. The German ships closed in on *Spearfish*, homing on her by using their detecting devices and plastering the area with depth charges which inflicted serious damage. Forbes was in a precarious position. The scars borne by *Spearfish* were such that he was obliged to consider the possibility of surfacing to scuttle. Every time he used his motors in a bid to slip away the enemy hydrophones found him and the depth charges rained down. But luck was with him. He detected the sound of a steamer passing overhead and, using her engines to cover the sound of his motors, he managed to slip the net of anti-submarine vessels. But his troubles were not over. Leaks in the high-pressure air lines had caused a critical build-up in pressure in the boat and Forbes realized that if he opened the hatch on the surface, the pressure inside the boat would cast him and several others clear out through the hatch. So when the boat finally surfaced, Forbes had to lash himself to the conning tower ladder and have a crewman hang on to his legs before he dared open the hatch. When the cover was opened the air in the boat shot up through the outlet and almost took Forbes with it. Had he not taken these precautions he would have been cast out to sea with the out-rush of air.

The refreshing air poured into the boat as she cruised along the surface recharging her batteries but the rest from trouble was not to last for long. One of the lookouts spotted a ship on the horizon and at first sight it was taken to be heading their way. Forbes dared not risk submerging with his batteries so low so he turned tail and headed away, but as he did so, a closer look at the ship on the horizon revealed that it was not heading their way but plunging through the waves away from them. Furthermore the ship was a big one – in fact the German pocket battleship *Lützow*. Already her captain had been warned of a submarine in the area but it was the *Triton* she had been warned of and was steering a wide course to avoid laying herself open to attack. Now she altered course again *en route* for Kiel but this alteration brought her into a position perfect for a salvo from *Spearfish*. Forbes did not miss the opportunity. Six torpedoes sliced through the water towards the unescorted pocket battleship. One of the 'fish' hit her in the stern, tearing her open and shattering her propellers and rudder and bringing her to a halt. She was taking in water fast and sat there at the mercy of the current, alone and unaided. Forbes, still on the surface and unaware that *Lützow* had no escort, beat a hasty retreat, bent on getting out of the area before he was subjected to another dose of depth charging.

Calls for help went out from *Lützow* but it wasn't until the following day that ships arrived and she was taken in tow. Three days later, after once running aground, she arrived at Kiel, where she remained for almost a year before she was fit for sea again. Forbes' attack had denied the Germans her use for that time and probably saved the lives of many merchantmen in the Atlantic for that was the mission planned for her after Kiel. Forbes was not to be around when *Lützow* was eventually put to sea again. In August 1940, *Spearfish* was sunk by another submarine, U-34, and all but one of her crew was lost.

In the period between the beginning of the German landings in Norway and Denmark and the end of the following month, British and Allied submarines accounted for almost 100,000 tons of enemy shipping, some of it scored by submarine mine-layers. But these successes were not achieved without loss. Four British submarines, the *Thistle*, *Tarpon*, *Sterlet* and *Unity*, were sunk by enemy action and the minelaying submarine *Seal* under the command of Lieutenant Commander Lonsdale was captured. The circumstances surrounding the loss of that last submarine caused uproar in the Submarine Service and the eventual court martial of her commanding officer.

Seal, while on a minelaying patrol in the Kattegat, suffered a violent explosion in a compartment in the after end of the boat and immediately took in water which flooded the compartment and drove the boat to the sea-bed. Lonsdale was in a difficult position. He dared not surface for it was still daylight and he therefore decided to lie low until night before making the attempt. When he estimated that night had come, Lonsdale ordered the main ballast tank blown but this had no sooner been done than the boat assumed a sharp bow-up angle. The weight of the water in the after compartment held it securely to the sea-bed. Movement in the boat at its steep angle became increasingly difficult, particularly when the air became foul. Throughout the night attempts were made to regain the buoyancy in the after compartment but to no avail. As work progressed it slowed up because of the lack of oxygen. By the following afternoon, no one on board was fit enough to do any more work. They had reached a stage of complete exhaustion but Lonsdale was resolved to make one last effort to surface. Before doing so, he sought the help of the Almighty and called the crew to prayer, but the crew was so exhausted that only a handful of them had the strength to crawl to the control room where Lonsdale held the service.

There was but one slim chance of survival and Lonsdale found it – a small amount of compressed air in an engine room bottle. This precious air was blown into the after tanks and, much to the surprise of everyone, the boat swept to the surface and the hatches were opened to let in fresh air. The crew had unquestionably been on the point of death. Had Lonsdale by his example and will-power not sustained morale and finally succeeded in surfacing, every one of them would have perished on the sea-bed. As it was, Lonsdale found himself on the surface in a boat which, although one engine was started, cruised in circles because of the damage to her after end. He had hoped to make a run for it and reach a neutral port but that was now out of the question. Lonsdale stopped the engine to review the situation but he had no sooner done so than a German Arado floatplane spotted the crippled submarine and charged in for an attack.

The floatplane roared in on the submarine with its machine-gun blazing and raked the bridge with fire. The bullets caught the First Lieutenant, the navigator and a rating and just missed Lonsdale. As the aircraft turned to attack once more, Lonsdale lowered the wounded men into the submarine. Round the floatplane came again but by now Lonsdale had a Lewis gun with which to reply and he pumped bullets at the plane until the magazine was empty.

With the firing ceased, the aeroplane touched down on the water nearby and a trawler pounded towards them. Lonsdale, realizing that there was no hope of escape, ordered all the secret books and equipment on board to be destroyed and the crew set about wrecking everything with all the strength they could muster. Scuttling the boat would have resulted in the loss of many lives for few of the men on board had the strength to swim and Lonsdale's prime concern was for the safety of his men.

When the aircraft had come to a halt, its pilot hailed the submarine and instructed someone to come over. Lonsdale, seeing an opportunity of gaining more time for his men to get about their work of wrecking the equipment, opted to go. He swam a short distance and reached the plane. By this time the trawler had arrived but by then the *Seal* was barely showing above water and all the equipment aboard her was truly destroyed so that even if they did succeed in getting her to port, the Germans would gain nothing by way of knowledge of their secret equipment.

After the war ended, Lieutenant Commander Lonsdale was court-martialled for allowing his submarine to fall into enemy hands. To a man, his crew stood loyally by him at the hearing. Every one of them owed his life to Lonsdale who along with them had been taken prisoner. Their captain, a courageous man whose first consideration had been for his crew, was honourably acquitted. When the verdict of the court was passed, his entire crew marched into the court room in tribute to their gallant commander.

With the German advance west across Europe, more sub-marines, notably Dutch, escaped to join Horton's force. The Submarine Service was growing in strength but as it grew, so the targets became fewer. The completion of the German Nor-wegian Campaign meant fewer enemy ships at large in the North Sea and a general intensification of anti-submarine activity down the Norwegian coastline made ventures in that area hazardous. Unlike their predecessors the Second World War submarine commanders had to cope with the possibility of air attack. The German Luftwaffe kept a vigilant watch over the Norwegian seas, scouring them for a hint of a submarine's presence. In spite of the increased perils, submarine operations continued in selected areas, such as the Skagerrak, on a reduced scale. It was during one such patrol that Lieutenant Com-mander Ben Bryant[1] had an 'argument' with an enemy ship, which almost brought his career as a submariner to an abrupt and fatal end.

Bryant, commander of the *Sealion*, was not to enjoy the good fortune shared by many of his compatriots in the campaign in Norwegian waters. His station in the Kattegat proved to be one fraught with hazard and on numerous occasions he and his crew were subjected to ferocious depth charge attacks, often resulting in *Sealion* barely managing to limp back to base. *Sealion*'s eighth patrol, which took place in August, was almost her last.

The patrol got off to a bad start when, patrolling at periscope depth, a U-boat was sighted only a few hundred yards away; a seemingly easy target, but before firing *Sealion* had to be brought round to bring her bow tubes to bear on the U-boat. She had no stern tubes. But by the time Bryant was in a firing position, the U-boat had altered course so that she was stern-on and presenting a slim target. Bryant fired a salvo but none of the torpedoes found their target. Determined to get his prey, he surfaced in the hope that he might get her with his deck gun but the U-boat commander merely dived to safety, out of harm's way.

It seemed that fate was being particularly fickle that night for some time later *Sealion*'s crew suffered the horror that all submariners dread when a mine scraped along the side of the casing while she was cruising on the surface. In the bridge the

[1] Later Rear-Admiral Ben Bryant, CBE, DSO and two bars, DSC.

watch stood riveted to the spot as it bumped its way along the length of the boat. No one could move. At any moment, there might be a shattering explosion, but luck was with them. The mine bumped off the casing for the last time and was swept away in the boat's wake.

Sealion was dogged by mechanical failure but despite these frustrating setbacks, Bryant chalked up a victory when he sent a German store ship to the bottom. Then two days later, he sighted a convoy of German transport ships under escort.

Bryant took *Sealion* down under the screen of destroyers and after suffering the annoyance of the convoy changing course just as he was about to fire a salvo, managed to get in a quick shot which sank the leading transport in the port column of ships. But immediately his troubles began. The tracks of the torpedoes had been seen and one of the transport ships made a smart change of course to ram *Sealion*. Bryant spotted the towering bows of the ship bearing down on him and gave the order to dive deep, but time was against him. As *Sealion* began to plunge nose-down into the depths, the bows of the transport caught her conning tower and cast her over on her side.

Inside the boat all was chaos as it was rammed over, casting the crew about and crashing them against instrument panels and myriad other pieces of machinery. The submarine continued to plummet downwards with the heavy forward ballast tanks flooded and she soared deeper than her maximum safe depth before a trim was regained. Even then as she squirmed away the depth charges sought her out. Luckily for Bryant and his crew, the Germans did not follow up the ramming with prolonged depth charging. They obviously imagined that the transport had delivered the *coup de grâce* and the attack was called off. When Bryant was finally able to bring *Sealion* to the surface he found that both of his periscope standards had been sheared off by the transport's bows and the conning tower was a tangle of wreckage. Had Bryant's dive not been quick enough they would all have perished. Fate, however, was preserving Bryant for more glorious deeds in other waters.

The threat of an invasion of the British Isles was heightened during the month of August when the Luftwaffe and the Royal Air Force became locked in combat. Goering, the Commander-in-Chief of the Luftwaffe, boasted that he could swat the RAF from the skies in a matter of days, and in so doing gain superiority which would allow Hitler's invasion forces to sweep across the Channel with comparative immunity. Goering had reckoned without the grit and determination of Britain's pilots. It quickly became clear that Goering's boasts of an early success were founded upon a mythological appreciation of the Luftwaffe's strength and destructive capability. Soon German bombers were being shot from the skies over southern England and the Channel and by mid-September, the Battle of Britain had reached its peak. The decisive day arrived on 15 September when the Luftwaffe took a mortal beating at the hands of the RAF and any thoughts Hitler had of invading Britain had to be swept aside.

Throughout this period, Horton had to reserve his submarines for anti-invasion combat in the event that an invasion might take place. It was clear that, if an invasion came, the submarine would play a crucial part in stemming the tide of enemy ships crossing the Channel. But now that that threat had been decisively removed by the RAF and the urgency of the hour passed, Horton could afford to give his submariners a well-earned rest. Throughout the protracted and trying campaign in Norwegian waters there had been little time for rest. Submarines remained at base only long enough to refuel and carry out such repairs as were necessary. Now the submariners could take a rest and fortify themselves for the fray. Horton too had an opportunity of turning his attentions in detail to the build-up of his submarine force. Improvements were designed for submarines already in the stocks. The building of the S-, T- and U-class submarines was stepped up.

The operational areas of the submarines were broadened to include the English Channel and the Bay of Biscay. With Hitler holding the Atlantic coast of France a close watch had to be kept on the ports situated there for it was clear that they would become important U-boat bases in the war of attrition in the Atlantic. Horton therefore directed a flotilla of submarines to stand guard over the Bay of Biscay while others sniped at the German shipping slipping along the Channel coast of France. But the German ships were well protected by escorts of fast patrol boats and aircraft from numerous bases along the northern coast of France. Successes were few but those that were achieved were thrust home with a determination typical of the Submarine Service.

By the end of the year submarine activity in the North Sea,

Channel and Bay of Biscay areas was reduced to routine patrols and with a few exceptions, it was to remain this way until the end of the war. This, however, by no means meant that the British submarine was out of the war – far from it. The situation had been hotting up in the blue waters of the Mediterranean and it was in this theatre of operation that some of the great events in British submarine history were to be enacted.

Italy entered the war on 10 June 1940 but two months earlier submarines had been slipping into the Mediterranean to reinforce the depleted force stationed there. When the war began, all but two of the British submarines stationed in the Mediterranean had been recalled for duties in the North Sea. With the likelihood of Italy's entry into the war on the side of Nazi Germany, the Admiralty had speedily begun a build-up of submarine strength. The situation had changed radically in that vast, land-locked sea. Until Italy's entry into the war, there had been no belligerent powers there and therefore no need for a strong sea-borne force. But now the complexion had swiftly changed.

Throughout the two months preceding Italy's declaration of war, the First Submarine Flotilla operating in the Mediterranean grew from two boats, which had originally been there for training purposes, to a force of twelve – six based at Malta and the other six based on the depot ship *Medway* at Alexandria. This handful of submarines against the Italian Navy, which comprised five capital ships, twenty-five cruisers, ninety destroyers and some ninety submarines.

The situation was tense. The British Mediterranean Fleet in no way matched the strength of the Italian Fleet and it therefore fell to the handful of submarines to carry out the first belligerent acts against the new foe. The Mediterranean was a vast area of sea to cover and with such a pitifully small submarine force it was impossible adequately to patrol it. The Commander-in-Chief therefore was obliged to concentrate his efforts in one area, where he reckoned the submarines would do most good. He chose to station them so as to hold good the communications in the Eastern Mediterranean and help sever the Italian supply routes in that area.

Immediately the Italians declared war, the British submarines took up their patrols to carry out their commander's orders; but in the first two weeks, they were struck by tragedy. Three submarines were lost from the Malta flotilla, the *Gram-*

pus, Odin and *Orpheus.* A fifty per cent loss in such a short time came as a bitter blow to the flotilla and one that could not be tolerated. But this was just the beginning. The Italians, with a powerful air force of almost 2,000 aircraft, launched an onslaught upon the tiny island of Malta, bent on razing her to the ground and therefore depriving the British Mediterranean Fleet of its submarine base there. Between the outbreak of war in the Mediterranean and the end of the month of June no fewer than fifty air raids were made on the base by Italian bombers; and the submarine base, which was open to attack from the air, took its fair share of the aerial bombardment, and indeed lost the submarine *Olympus* when she was hit by a bomb while undergoing a refit in dry dock.

These severe losses were in some way compensated for by the success of Lieutenant Commander Rimington, in the submarine *Parthian*, when he sank the Italian submarine *Diamante*. But successes such as this were few and the next victory scored was tinged with sadness. Lieutenant Commander J. W. Linton, a captain destined to rank among the 'greats' in the Mediterranean, commander of the P-class boat *Pandora*, was patrolling off the coast of Algiers, his mission to prevent ships of the French Fleet falling into German hands. His orders were to sink any French warships he encountered lest they reach France and become part of the German Navy.

It ought to be explained that by this time the Armistice between France and Germany had been signed and there was considerable concern at the Admiralty that ships of the French Fleet might fall into German hands and therefore reinforce her surface fleet. The balance of naval power in the Mediterranean was weighted heavily enough against the Royal Navy without the chance of additional naval units supplementing the enemy force. The decision to sink French ships was a grim one, but in the light of the Mediterranean situation, it had to be taken. Linton's career as an 'ace' in the Mediterranean was to begin with such an encounter when he sighted the French minelaying sloop *Rigault de Genoully* on 4 July. Linton put three torpedoes into her and she sank.

The Mediterranean situation was steadily worsening. Towards the end of July Italian convoys began to sail from Italy to Libya, ferrying troops and munitions in preparation for Mussolini's attack on Egypt. The British army in Egypt was simply not equipped in fighting manpower or in suitable weapons to undertake a defence of the country which housed the crucial Suez canal, the man-made sea-way through which British ships from India, Australia and the Far East passed. To lose Egypt would result in a virtual strangulation of troop movements between the far-reaching points of the Commonwealth.

It was abundantly clear that, to fight such a war, Mussolini would have to count upon an uninterrupted flow of supplies across the Mediterranean – but who was to stop him? Malta, sitting as it does in the central Mediterranean basin, was an ideal base from which to operate a fleet against the Italian supply routes; but she was so heavily bombarded by the Italian air force that she was unable to function properly as either a naval or air base. Her defences were abysmally poor and therefore she could not reply to the day-and-night bombing wrought upon her. The onus lay upon Britain's submarines – and there were few enough of these to take on such a formidable opponent.

The battle for North Africa began in earnest in September 1940, when the Italians attempted an invasion of Egypt and the long, drawn-out war for control of the Mediterranean 'hotted up' to a fiendish pace. Among the naval forces there were losses on both sides. While British submarine successes against merchant shipping leapt up, so also did their losses; and in the period from the beginning of the war with Italy to the end of the year, the Royal Navy lost nine submarines. The cost was high and the results did not merit such fearful loss of life and boats. The lack of appreciable success was due in no small measure to insufficient aerial reconnaissance. Good aerial cover would have pin-pointed the Italian convoys and the submarines and surface ships could have 'homed' on them, and perhaps the results might have been better. But as it was, Malta, the base from which reconnaissance sorties could be flown, was sadly lacking in long-range aircraft and the personnel to man them, despite valiant missions by submarines to ferry personnel in and reinforce the weakened air force strength. Such were the adverse conditions under which British submarines had to operate; but under these tortuous conditions men were to achieve fame, victory and immortality in their submarines; men like Wanklyn, Miers, Roberts, Gould and Linton, to name only a handful. It was in 1941 that these men showed their prowess, skill and courage, when the odds were at their worst.

To do justice to the exploits of the British submarines in the Mediterranean theatre would take more than one volume. Space does not allow a detailed account of the many successes and tragedies suffered by these submarines. However, the accounts that follow exemplify the courage and determination of all the submariners who fought in that theatre where some of the war's most bitter fighting took place.

In January of 1941, the build-up of submarines in the Mediterranean began to move with increased momentum. The First, Eighth and Tenth Flotillas comprised the fighting submarine strength of the Mediterranean. The First, operating in the eastern end of the sea from the depot ship *Medway*, was growing, and by the middle of the year had five T-class, three R-class, two P-class and one O-class submarines as well as the minelayer *Cachalot*. The Eighth Flotilla, based on Gibraltar at the opposite end of the Mediterranean, acted as a working-up flotilla for Mediterranean operations and also for convoy escort duties. Until the end of March, this flotilla, operating as it did from a shore base, finally got its depot ship, HMS *Maidstone*. The Tenth Flotilla, operating out of the beleaguered island of Malta, had only four U-class submarines at the beginning of the year but in the first six months this force was increased by six more submarines of the same class.

January saw the arrival at Malta of the man who has been hailed as the greatest submarine commander of the Second World War, Lieutenant Commander Malcolm David Wanklyn, RN. He was captain of the U-class boat *Upholder*, in which he and his crew were to bring destruction upon Axis shipping in the Mediterranean. *Upholder* was a brand new boat, having just completed her 'working-up' period before arriving at Malta. Wanklyn was, however, no newcomer to submarines. He volunteered for the Silent Service in 1933 after distinguishing himself at the Royal Navy College, Dartmouth. He was tall – almost too tall for submarines, topping six feet, and sported a handsome black beard; a man who, because of an inherent quality, commanded the respect and unflinching loyalty of all who served with him.

Before taking up command of *Upholder*, Wanklyn had already done his share of patrols in the North Sea and for a time served as First Lieutenant of the submarine *Porpoise* under the command of the man who was now Commander

(Submarines) Malta, Commander G. W. G. 'Shrimp' Simpson.[1] Simpson had noted all Wanklyn's qualities as an officer and was delighted when he was sent to join his flotilla. He expected great things of the young submarine commander – but, alas, Wanklyn's first patrols which began on 24 January were to be a disappointment and showed nothing of the greatness he was destined to achieve.

Upholder sailed from Malta and took up her patrol line off the coast of Tunisia, near what is known as the Kerkenah Bank. Every submariner's mind was dogged by the thought that every torpedo must count. Because of the virtual siege and continuous bombardment of Malta, there was an acute shortage of torpedoes on the island and, indeed, orders were issued to the effect that torpedoes should be used only on those enemy ships which were actually heading for North Africa, carrying fresh troops and supplies. Torpedoes were not to be 'wasted' on outward-bound ships from North Africa which were in all probability empty. Commanders therefore had to be 'choosey' about which enemy ships they decided to attack.

Wanklyn's chance of a victory came only two days out from Malta, while surfaced and recharging his batteries. Shortly after 0100 hours on the 26th, a supply ship, escorted by a destroyer, was sighted and Wanklyn made a long-range surface attack, firing two torpedoes. But the range was too great and the supply ship caught sight of the torpedoes and easily evaded them. Meanwhile the destroyer swung in to attack *Upholder* and Wanklyn scurried away out of danger. Shortly after, he sighted another supply ship and again launched a long-range attack but alas with similar results. Both torpedoes missed. These encounters were a singularly inglorious start to Wanklyn's war in the Mediterranean. Already he had expended four valuable torpedoes without even hitting an enemy ship, let alone inflicting any damage.

When the next opportunity came, however, Wanklyn was not content with firing from far off. Two days after his unsuccessful attack on the supply ships, he sighted another two supply ships and this time, wiser after the failure of his previous encounter, he closed to 900 yards before firing his torpedoes. The subsequent explosion which resounded across the water to *Upholder* came as music to the ears of Wanklyn and her crew. The 8,000-ton German transport *Duisburg* settled down in the

[1] Later Rear-Admiral G. W. G. Simpson, CB, CBE.

water, mortally wounded by Wanklyn's torpedoes. Three days later, he sent another enemy transport to the bottom out of a protected convoy but was immediately subjected to a fearful depth charge attack. Only Wanklyn's masterly skill of prediction, 'reading' the enemy's mind, coupled with the expert use of his Asdic saved the boat from destruction at the hands of determined hunters.

Wanklyn brought *Upholder* back to Malta on 1 February at the height of an air raid. These aerial onslaughts were becoming part of the daily routine on the island and at one point reached a state where she was subjected to continuous bombardment for twelve of the twenty-four hours of the day, by both Italian and German aircraft. 'Shrimp' Simpson greeted Wanklyn and congratulated him on his first successes in that theatre. His patrol, although it had not begun successfully, had ended in victory.

The element of luck plays a critical part in a submarine commander's life but the luck which had attended Wanklyn in the latter part of his first patrol was not to be with him during the few that were to follow. Indeed, his negative returns were to cast doubt in the minds of his superiors as to his suitability as a commander. Even Simpson, who had implicit faith in Wanklyn's ability, was to have the seeds of doubt sown in his mind when, on his next four patrols, Wanklyn was to put up a 'poor' performance.

Buoyant after their two notable successes on the first patrol, Wanklyn and the crew of *Upholder* left Malta on 12 February in confident mood to take up patrol again in the same area, off the Kerkenah Bank. While heading for the patrol area, another submarine was sighted and the first thought was that it might be Italian. Wanklyn closed on it but recognized it as a T-class British submarine. However two things were odd about her. The first was that Wanklyn had had no warning of her presence in that area and secondly she refused to answer Wanklyn's challenge. Could it be, Wanklyn thought, that he had been wrong in his identification and it was an enemy submarine and therefore a very worthwhile target? Wanklyn would have been justified in attacking since the submarine failed to answer his challenge and identify herself but instead he let her proceed unharmed. It is as well that he did, for the submarine was none other than *Truant* which had been forced to return to base because her radio was out of action. The upshot of the incident might have had tragic consequences had not Wanklyn been so positive of his ability at recognition.

The patrol passed without sight of many enemy ships but one attack was carried out, and although Wanklyn manoeuvred into an ideal firing position none of his torpedoes found the mark. This unfortunate miss was to herald a lengthy train of such events. Disappointed, Wanklyn brought *Upholder* back with an empty bag. The same sad result attended the two patrols that followed during the month of March. The second of these patrols was carried out off the coast of Sicily and he brought back some valuable reconnaissance information but that could not compensate for the lack of success in sinking enemy ships. Worse was to come....

On his fifth patrol in April Wanklyn found three good targets, expended a total of eight torpedoes and not one of them scored a hit. This, in the light of the acute torpedo shortage in Malta, was enough to cloud a man's reputation but not Wanklyn's. Outwardly at least, he showed no signs of the bitter disappointment he must have felt. There did, however, come an incident which in its way showed clearly Wanklyn's spark of genius. Returning from this patrol with all his torpedoes expended, he sighted an enemy convoy south-bound for North Africa. Realizing that he could not strike, and being aware as he was that there were British surface vessels not too far off, he pulled off a master stroke. The enemy must, he reasoned, be aware that there were British surface warships not far off. Wanklyn closed up his guns crew and fired a series of star shells. His ruse worked. The enemy captains, thinking that the star shells were a signal for a surface attack, turned tail and headed back to base rather than face the possibility of an encounter with British warships. If nothing else, Wanklyn had at least temporarily delayed the flow of vital supplies to Rommel's army in North Africa. But even this was not enough. There were serious mutterings as to the competency of a commander who 'wasted' eight torpedoes without result. But if Wanklyn's superiors had their doubts, his crew never for a moment had anything short of complete and implicit faith in his ability as a commander – such was the calibre of the man.

What had happened to the man who had showed such great promise? This was the question which puzzled his superiors; but if it gave them cause for concern it was an even greater worry to Wanklyn himself who must have spent his every waking hour pondering the subject of his inability to exorcise the spectre of bad luck which had haunted him. Wanklyn was in no doubt that his next patrol, the sixth, would be a critical one for him as a commander. He went about the preparations for the patrol with his usual meticulous precision, determined not to allow the run of ill-luck to deviate him from his course.

Upholder sailed on 21 April and three days later sighted a convoy off Kerkenah Bank. Wanklyn selected the 5,428-ton *Antonietta Laura* as his target, closed to 700 yards, and dispatched her to the bottom of the sea. The spell had been broken, and the following day he proved that that had been no fleeting moment of good luck. Wanklyn received orders to proceed to the Kerkenah Bank where an enemy destroyer had got herself run aground. The water was shallow and Wanklyn knew only too well that during the attack, which would have to be carried out on the surface, there would be no depth for diving should trouble arrive, either from the air or from the sea. Wanklyn therefore decided to bide his time and wait for late afternoon before launching his attack. By doing this he would be able to withdraw under cover of darkness.

When he finally slipped towards his target he found the destroyer *and* a supply ship, the *Arta*, stuck fast on the bank. But as *Upholder* proceeded towards the two targets, she too ran aground but managed to free herself. Wanklyn, with the thought of 'wasted' torpedoes ringing in his ears, guessed that a 'fish' fired at the destroyer would probably get stuck in the sand bank. Wanklyn decided to ignore the deserted and abandoned warship and concentrate upon the *Arta*. He sent a boarding party aboard and, after blowing the ship's safe, set demolition charges and retired to watch the effect. Soon the ship was ablaze from stem to stern.

Upholder's patrol continued and on 1 May while patrolling at periscope depth Wanklyn got the call to go to the control room. The hydrophone had picked up propeller noises and they were getting louder, indicating ships coming their way. Wanklyn, who had been snatching one of the few brief rests a submarine commander allows himself on patrol, hurried to the control room, where he found a flurry of activity. Through the periscope he could make out masts on the horizon. As the minutes passed, the objects on the horizon grew more discernible – an enemy convoy was steaming his way. It comprised five transports, escorted by four destroyers.

With his usual precision, Wanklyn calmly issued the orders that brought the crew to action stations. All four bow tubes were loaded as he brought *Upholder* into firing position. Everyone went about his job with practised efficiency and Wanklyn fired a full salvo of four torpedoes, then brought down the periscope and waited. These intervening minutes were the most anxious. Then they came, three resounding crunches as all but one of his 'fish' hit their targets. Two torpedoes found the 6,000-ton German transport *Arcturus* while the third hit and damaged the 7,386-ton motor-ship *Leverkusen*. Wanklyn ordered 'up periscope' and surveyed the scene. *Arcturus* was sinking fast but the other ship had only stopped, obviously just damaged. Already the destroyers were racing in on him for the kill and Wanklyn took *Upholder* deep until the depth charge attack was over. Then he brought her to periscope depth and with the skill and daring that was to mark the rest of his career, Wanklyn used his last torpedo to hit and sink the crippled *Leverkusen*. With all his torpedoes expended, he returned to Malta to a joyous – and relieved – 'Shrimp' Simpson, whose faith in Wanklyn had finally been justified.

The burst of success enjoyed by Wanklyn and *Upholder* on that sixth, and crucial, patrol was no 'flash in the pan', as he was to demonstrate on their next foray in the Mediterranean. This time his patrol area was changed. He was ordered to the east coast of Sicily to attack enemy convoys coming out of the Straits of Messina but the patrol got off to a bad start and one that might well have tempted a lesser commander to abort the patrol and return to base.

Wanklyn sighted a small convoy and launched an attack but it failed and brought upon him a ferocious counter-attack by escorting destroyers. Depth charge explosions wrecked the Asdic gear. This was critical for its loss seriously impaired the fighting efficiency of the boat.

On two successive days and in spite of the unserviceable Asdic, Wanklyn delivered attacks on two convoys on 22 and 23 May, sinking two ships. But after the second attack he underwent a fierce counter-attack during which the bow-cap of a torpedo tube was damaged, making that tube incapable of operation. Now he had only two torpedoes left, one of which was in the damaged tube. This had to be transferred to another tube, ready for action. The submarine was hardly what one might describe as 'serviceable' but, resolutely, Wanklyn con-

tinued his patrol, determined to use the remaining two torpedoes to maximum effect. And he did, for on the evening of
24 May, in foul weather conditions which made periscope observation extremely difficult, he sighted an Italian convoy,
comprising four of the enemy's finest ocean liners, the *Marco
Polo, Victoria, Esperia* and *Conte Rosso*. It was clear that they
were carrying valuable cargoes. In a 'crippled' submarine, with
only two torpedoes remaining, Wanklyn prepared to attack.
This could only be the classic 'David and Goliath' touch. For
the attack which was about to take place, Wanklyn was awarded
the Submarine Service's first Victoria Cross of the Second World
War. The citation read:

'On the evening of the 24th May 1941, while on patrol off
the coast of Sicily, Lieutenant Commander Wanklyn, in His
Majesty's Submarine *Upholder*, sighted a southbound enemy
troop convoy, strongly escorted by destroyers.

'The failing light was such that observation by periscope
could not be relied on, but a surface attack would have been
easily seen. *Upholder*'s listening gear was out of action.

'In spite of these handicaps, Lieutenant Commander
Wanklyn decided to press home his attack at short range. He
quickly steered his craft into a favourable position and closed
in so as to make sure of his target. By this time the where-
abouts of the escorting destroyers could not be made out.
Lieutenant Commander Wanklyn, while fully aware of the
risk of being rammed by one of the escorts, continued to
press on towards the enemy troopships. As he was about to
fire, one of the enemy destroyers suddenly appeared out of
the darkness at high speed and he only just avoided being
rammed. As soon as he was clear, he brought his periscope
sights on and fired torpedoes, which sank a large troopship.
The enemy destroyers at once made a strong counter-attack
and during the next 20 minutes dropped 37 depth charges
near *Upholder*.

'The failure of his listening device made it much harder
for him to get away but with the greatest courage, coolness
and skill, he brought *Upholder* clear of the enemy and safe
back to harbour.'

Official citations are of necessity brief and to the point. The
troopship which Wanklyn had sunk was the 18,000-ton *Conte*

Rosso, crammed with troops bound for North Africa, and he had sunk her at an estimated speed of twenty knots. This, coupled with the factor that he could hardly see his target, and was at the moment before firing forced to veer out of the way of a destroyer's bow then take a 'snap' shot at her, adds to the brilliance of the attack. The attack alone warranted the highest praise, but the way in which he managed to negotiate his boat out of trouble only went to highlight the sheer genius of this man – one who, without any means of determining where his attackers were, was able to predict their moves with uncanny foresight.

The triumphant reception back at base was marred by an unfortunate accident which occurred when torpedoes were being loaded into *Upholder* in preparation for the next patrol. For some inexplicable reason, one of the torpedoes which was being loaded into its tube began to run and instantly gave off poisonous carbon-monoxide. Petty Officer Carter tried desperately to shut off the torpedo but was overcome by the fumes and collapsed. Lieutenant Read, the torpedo officer, also tried to stop the torpedo's engine but he too was overcome. Both men were eventually rescued and rushed to hospital suffering from severe carbon-monoxide poisoning – even in dock there were risks to be run.

There was little rest for Wanklyn and his crew but, despite the strain, *Upholder* continued to achieve considerable victories, adding further transports to her already handsome list of successes. Two of them fell to torpedoes and the Italian cruiser *Garibaldi* was severely damaged in one of Wanklyn's typically brilliant attacks. He had at the time only two torpedoes left and the Italian was streaking through the water at twenty-eight knots. Wanklyn realized that if he hesitated for a moment the cruiser would be there and gone before he'd a chance to fire. With his brain working like a computer, he swung the boat around and in a scant few minutes he'd put two torpedoes into her. These, alas, were not enough to sink her but they caused severe damage. *Upholder* again was subjected to fierce reprisals but escaped unscathed.

On her twelfth patrol, in mid-August, Wanklyn embarked some army passengers and was ordered to take them on a special mission to Palermo on the north coast of Sicily. Wanklyn's passengers were, however, to get a taste of action in a submarine before they were delivered. The 852-ton trawler *Enotria* went to the bottom after having been hit by two of *Upholder*'s torpedoes. Then some days later, when a convoy was sighted, Wanklyn claimed another victim when he sank a 4,500-ton tanker. To cap that he sighted a strong naval surface force consisting of a battleship, two cruisers and several destroyers. Finding himself again with only two torpedoes left, he attacked a cruiser but was unable to confirm a hit because of a ferocious depth charge attack which followed. The army officer and his corporal withstood the depth charge well but it was with no mean relief that they clambered into their canoe on the night of 25 August and paddled off on their mission to blow up a railway line. The arrangement was that Wanklyn would lie in wait for the raiders until their mission was complete then pick them up and ferry them back to base.

Not long after they had left, however, there was a burst of activity near the shore. Shots were fired and Wanklyn guessed that the two men had been captured. But true to his promise, he waited until at last the two men returned. They had failed to achieve their objective because of a very steep climb. To find another route to the railway would have meant being late for their rendezvous so rather than risk capture they returned to the submarine to try again another day.

Wanklyn brought the two army men back to base but if either he or any of his crew imagined they were in for a well-earned respite, they were mistaken. Only forty-eight hours after returning to Malta *Upholder* was ordered to sea again. Intelligence had reported a large enemy convoy of three troopships, heavily escorted by destroyers. On the last day of August, Wanklyn sighted the enemy convoy but although he made a determined attack, none of his torpedoes found the mark and he was forced to return to base 'empty-handed'.

Upholder had successfully escaped numerous depth charge attacks and she was regarded as a 'lucky' boat both by her crew and others. Other Malta-based boats were not so lucky. The submarine *Usk* was lost in April, *Undaunted* in May, *Union* in July and P-32 and P-33 in August. The odds indeed were heavily stacked against the British submarines for the Axis forces had virtual air supremacy and by rights should have ruled the Mediterranean Sea. Particularly troublesome to the submarines were the extensive enemy minefields laid by the Italians in the central Mediterranean. The enemy knew the way through them, but the British did not and it is likely that some of the boats lost by the Malta Flotilla succumbed to these horned devils. The Italians had also developed small but very fast boats which could 'pounce' on a submarine while it was re-charging its batteries and catch it unawares on the surface before it had time to dive. These hazards, plus the fatigue of patrols lasting a fortnight at a time, made submarine operation in the Mediterranean the perilous pursuit it was.

Wanklyn, like everyone else in submarines, was all too aware of these myriad difficulties in prosecuting the submarine war but on the surface at least he remained the calm, unruffled commander who, it seemed, had both skill and luck on his side. He demonstrated this deadly combination on his next sortie which was undertaken in concert with three other submarines, *Unbeaten*, *Urge* and *Upright*.

The four submarines left Malta in mid-September to lay a trap for a convoy of Italian liners which, air reconnaissance had reported, had left the Italian naval base at Taranto the previous day and were steaming under escort for Tripoli. The four sub-marines were to lie in ambush for the liners, the *Neptunia*, *Oceania* and *Vulcania*.

As she raced to her allotted position, *Upholder* suffered a set-back – her gyro-compass became unserviceable and therefore Wanklyn had to rely upon the magnetic compass for navigation. Determined as ever, Wanklyn pressed on.

Early in the morning *Unbeaten* sighted the convoy, but she was too far off to attack and radioed the others to warn them of its approach. Just before 4 a.m., Wanklyn in *Upholder* caught sight of the towering masts of the liners and manoeuvred at full speed on the surface to get into attacking position. He noticed that there were three large two-funnelled liners, escorted by six destroyers. His timing was perfection itself, despite a sea which forced his bows to adopt a yawing movement. As the bows rode to-and-fro Wanklyn took advantage of the swing. *Upholder* was so positioned that at the crucial firing point, two of the liners 'overlapped', presenting a long, continuous target. The first torpedo Wanklyn fired was aimed at the bows of the lead ship, the second at the stern of the other liner and the third and fourth slap in the middle of the solid 'wall' of steel.

Anticipating a swift counter-attack, Wanklyn took *Upholder* deep and waited. Then came the truth-telling thuds as at least two of his 'fish' slammed into the targets. Complete silence was observed in *Upholder* in the tense minutes that followed the reverberating explosions, but the Italian escorts sought no retribution and after almost an hour's wait, Wanklyn thought it safe to bring *Upholder* to periscope depth. The sight that met his eyes as he stared into the periscope filled him with satisfaction, for one of the liners, the *Neptunia*, had sunk; the *Vulcania* had fled the scene; and the other, the *Oceania*, was stopped and obviously damaged.

Although Wanklyn was gratified that his torpedoes had caught their targets, he was, as always at times like these, heartsick at the thought of the men who had gone to the bottom. Wanklyn, in spite of his great professional skill as a submariner, was a sensitive man with an ingrained dislike of killing, although he never allowed this to affect his judgement of his role as a hunter. He knew only too well that every ship he sunk brought the chances of victory closer and went a long way to saving countless Allied lives in North Africa.

There was, however, little time for emotional reflections as he studied the scene through the periscope. The *Oceania*, with the destroyers fussing around her in a protective screen, had to be finished off. Wanklyn took *Upholder* down to reload torpedoes and prepare for the attack. When dawn came he brought her to periscope depth and prepared to fire but just as he was about to do so, an Italian destroyer bore down on the submarine and Wanklyn had to dive out of the way of her bows. When he brought her up again he found himself in an unsuitable position from which to fire his torpedoes so he took *Upholder* right under the liner and up to periscope depth on the other side. He swung her around and fired two torpedoes. Both of them hit the crippled ship and she sank, much to the consternation and amazement of Lieutenant Commander Woodward, in *Unbeaten*, who had arrived in the area and was about to fire a salvo at the ship when it was hit and disappeared before his eyes.

In that attack, Wanklyn had accounted for no less than 39,000 tons of Italian shipping and many troops, as well as forcing the other liner to flee back from whence she had come. The ambush had worked.

Such was the success rate of the Malta submarines that the Axis powers were seriously worried – so worried in fact that Malta was subjected to an even more intensified barrage and the aircraft concentrated their bombs where it would hurt most – on the submarine anchorages and dock-yard; but fortunately *Upholder* escaped unscathed.

Wanklyn's victories mounted as patrols continued throughout the remainder of the year. He had few chances for respite from the nerve-racking job of commanding his submarine but in spite of the constant submission to tension he remained, outwardly at least, calm and efficient, never allowing himself to succumb to the fatigue that such an arduous task entailed.

On his seventeenth patrol in Mediterranean waters, Wanklyn sank an Italian submarine with a salvo of torpedoes and the following day accounted for the Italian destroyer *Libeccio*. Only a few hours had passed when he attacked a group of enemy warships and seriously damaged another destroyer. The patrol lasted only four days but in that short time Wanklyn had 'notched up' a noteworthy score in Italian warships.

Upholder came very close to being lost while on a day exercise in December under the command of Lieutenant Norman. When returning to harbour she was 'jumped' by German fighters which raked her with cannon fire. Lieutenant Norman on the bridge was hit several times and collapsed and fell down the conning tower into the control room before the hatch could be secured. Already the submarine was beginning her dive and he bravely managed to struggle up the ladder and secure the hatch before the water covered it – in spite of terrible wounds. Had he not done so, *Upholder* would have been swamped with sea and in all probability lost.

Upholder had suffered only one of many lightning strikes carried out by enemy fighters in a bid to catch the submarines napping on the surface as they entered or left harbour. The form from then on was to dive before leaving or entering harbour, a tricky operation even when carried out by skilled commanders.

The Scots on board *Upholder* were denied their traditional New Year's celebration for she sailed on patrol on 31 December. On 4 January Wanklyn sighted the 5,000-ton *Sirio* and fired two torpedoes at her. One of the torpedoes dropped to the seabed and exploded almost directly beneath *Upholder* but she sustained only slight damage and not enough to affect the patrol. A further two torpedoes were fired at the enemy ship but only one hit, crippling her. Still she would not sink and Wanklyn surfaced to engage her with his deck gun, but the gallant crew of the enemy ship opened up at *Upholder* with such intense fire that Wanklyn had to break off the action and retreat.

The following morning brought fresh fodder for *Upholder* but by then Wanklyn had only one torpedo left. He sighted the Italian submarine *Ammiraglio St Bon* while both submarines were on the surface. He noticed that her guns crew was closing up, so he dived and fired his sole remaining torpedo. That was enough to send the enemy submarine to the bottom with only three survivors.

Wanklyn's next patrol off the Italian naval base of Taranto proved fruitless, a most unusual occurrence for the great commander when he returned with a full load of torpedoes. 'Shrimp' Simpson, by then a full captain in command of the Tenth Flotilla, sensed the enormous strain under which Wanklyn was operating and ordered him to take a rest; so towards the end of January, he was sent off to a rest camp for a well deserved respite while *Upholder* was taken on patrol by Lieutenant Norman. During the patrol Norman sank a 2,500-ton ship.

Rested after his short break from operations, Wanklyn took *Upholder* on her twenty-third patrol on 21 February and six days later sank the 5,500-ton *Tembien* with two torpedoes.

Losses among the Malta Flotilla mounted rapidly during the early months of 1942 and most of these were sustained under air attack while at base. The full weight of the enemy air force was concentrated against the island and four of the U-class submarines at the base were seriously damaged, two of them beyond repair. In addition to these, the Greek submarine *Glavkos* was sunk while the Polish *Sokol* was hit several times by bombs. *Pandora*, the submarine which had been ferrying spares into Malta, was destroyed by bombs and sunk while unloading, but in a successful recovery operation some of her torpedoes were retrieved and later used. As well as these losses at Malta, P-38 did not return from patrol. It seemed that the Malta Flotilla would be unable to continue operations but in spite of these reverses among her sister ships, *Upholder* remained a 'lucky' boat.

On his twenty-fourth patrol, Wanklyn was sent for the first time to the Adriatic where he sank yet another Italian submarine and a trawler which he sent to the bottom by gun-fire. Following this, *Upholder* was diverted back to keep watch over Taranto and although he sighted a battleship and attacked, none of his torpedoes found their mark. Without any 'teeth' left, Wanklyn brought *Upholder* back to Malta.

Upholder had by then been operational for sixteen months and was due for a complete refit in England in April. Wanklyn, determined to stay in the thick of the fighting, pleaded with Captain Simpson to allow him to take over command of another submarine; but Simpson would have none of it – home he was going. But he was to carry out one final patrol – the twenty-fifth – before taking *Upholder* back to England. She left Malta on 6 April to land some agents on the North African coast. This part of the mission was completed successfully and on the night of 11 April, *Upholder* rendezvoused with *Unbeaten* to transfer an army officer; then the two submarines parted company, with *Upholder* heading for a patrol line off Tripoli, where a big Italian convoy was expected to arrive.

On 14 April, *Upholder*'s sister ship, *Urge*, heard heavy depth charging in the vicinity of the position where *Upholder* was thought to be. The Italian torpedo boat *Pegaso* had made contact with a submarine and launched an intensive depth charge attack. After only fifteen minutes of the attack, the submarine was no longer heard on the listening device on board the Italian boat. Wanklyn had failed to evade the murderous depth charges and he and his entire crew were lost.

Over the days that followed signals were repeatedly sent out to *Upholder* in the hope that she might answer, but none came. It was clear that *Upholder* had met its fate; but everyone in the flotilla refused to believe it had happened. They were numbed by the shock of the loss of this boat which, apart from its brilliant success, had been an inspiration to everyone on the beleaguered island. So devastating was the news of the loss, that for some weeks it was not announced officially that *Upholder* was gone. Only Wanklyn's relatives were told. Then the Admiralty took an almost unique step in issuing a special communiqué. It read:

'It is seldom proper for Their Lordships to draw distinctions between different services rendered in the course of naval duty, but they take this opportunity of singling out those of HMS *Upholder*, under the command of Lieutenant Commander Wanklyn, for special mention. She was long employed against enemy communications in the Central Mediterranean, and she became noted for the uniformly high quality of her services in that arduous and dangerous duty. Such was the standard of skill and daring, that the ship and her officers and men became an inspiration not only to their own flotilla but to the fleet of which it was a part, and Malta, where for so long HMS *Upholder* was based. The ship and her company are gone but the example and the inspiration remains.'

The Royal Navy had lost a brilliant submarine commander and one who, had his life been spared, would have unquestionably risen to the highest ranks of the service. In the course of its sixteen months of operation in the Mediterranean, Wanklyn's boat had accounted for three U-boats and one destroyer sunk, one cruiser and one destroyer and nineteen transport ships either damaged or sunk; a total of 119,000 tons. No other British commander was to equal that score but that is not to say that they did not go about their job with all the resolution, cunning and courage shown by Wanklyn. The name of Lieutenant Commander John Wallace Linton ranks as high as that of the great Wanklyn in the immortals of the Submarine Service.

As was seen earlier, Tubby Linton, commanding the P-class submarine *Pandora*, drew 'first blood' in the Mediterranean when she sank the Vichy French sloop *Rigault de Genoully*, off the coast of Algiers on 3 July 1940, shortly after her arrival in the Mediterranean. The P-class *Pandora* was a veritable giant of a submarine compared with Wanklyn's U-class boat. It was over 2,000 tons in displacement, old, difficult to handle and too big for operations in the shallow waters of the North Sea. It was for this latter reason that, upon the outbreak of war, she was not immediately recalled from China where she was stationed at the time. When Italy entered the war, however, and there came a desperate need for submarines in the Mediterranean she, along with others of the Far East boats of the same class, was urgently ordered to make for the Mediterranean, and she joined the First Submarine Flotilla at Alexandria.

Linton was a strong, robust officer; precise, determined and respected by his crew. He commanded a happy ship, with a crew which had every confidence in its commander. But it was not the boat in which Linton was destined to gain distinction, although she carried out some invaluable work, particularly in running the gauntlet of the enemy air and sea forces by ferrying supplies into the beleaguered Malta. *Pandora* was, by the middle of 1941, long overdue for a complete overhaul; and she was sent to America to undergo this lengthy refit. Linton, however, did not go with her. He took command of a brand-new T-class submarine, the *Turbulent*, in November 1941 and it was in this boat that Linton was to become one of the great submariners of the Second World War.

Linton brought *Turbulent* to the Mediterranean in January 1942 and, after working-up at Gibraltar, arrived at Alexandria the following month to join the First Flotilla. (In April, Linton's previous command, *Pandora*, was sunk while off-loading valuable supplies at Malta.)

Linton lost no time in chalking up a handsome score. In his second patrol in *Turbulent*, he sank six small ships using his deck gun and only narrowly escaped destruction when shortly after he attacked a convoy and came under ferocious depth charge attack.

Linton's area of operation in the eastern Mediterranean and the Aegean Sea was to prove a fruitful hunting ground. During his fourth patrol, when only three days out of Alexandria, he sank a schooner which was loaded to the gunwales with ammunition. The resulting explosion had a heartening effect upon Linton's crew but the celebrations were short-lived for an enemy aircraft swept down on *Turbulent* and forced her to dive.

17 May saw *Turbulent* cruising on the surface when Linton sighted a convoy of two enemy ships under destroyer escort. It was a dark night and Linton used the mantle of darkness to sneak in astern of the convoy and keep watch on it. The low conning tower of the submarine was unseen by the Italians against the dark sea and Linton trailed the convoy, watching the pattern of its movements and choosing just the right moment for the attack. When he thought the time was right, he pushed on some power and slipped up to the beam of the convoy and turned to attack; but he wasn't satisfied with his firing position so, with the patience of Job, he repeated the performance and the second time found himself ideally situated.

Three torpedoes streaked out of *Turbulent*'s tubes and two of them scored hits; but within seconds the destroyer was wheeling round and bearing down fast on the submarine. Linton, a bulky man in stature, struggled down through the topmost conning tower hatch but found that it would not close properly. Leaving it he scrambled down through the second hatch into the control room as the submarine dived beneath the waves and went about the business of avoiding the depth charging that followed. When *Turbulent* surfaced an hour later, the upper conning tower was flooded and Linton had to emerge through the gun tower hatch.

Seven days later, she had another close shave when an enemy bomber unloaded a cluster of bombs which straddled the submarine but luckily did no damage. Only forty-eight hours after that narrow escape, she was subjected to yet another depth charge attack when she attacked an enemy convoy and was spotted by a destroyer. Far from demoralizing Linton and his crew this harassment merely made them all the more determined to exact revenge upon the enemy.

The following night, while surfaced with diesel engines running and batteries recharging, Linton's lookouts spotted flares, far off on the horizon; but from whence they came was a mystery for there was a low mist. An hour later, Linton, on the bridge, caught sight of a small convoy consisting of two supply ships under escort by two destroyers. The mist was an annoyance for it made the possibility of an attack difficult. Linton therefore decided to bide his time and wait for morning before launching his attack. He manoeuvred his boat into a position whereby he could keep watch over the convoy until the time was ripe for attack. Keeping such a position was difficult, for the convoy was steaming an irregular zig-zag course, changing its course without warning.

By 2.30 a.m., the mist had all but cleared and the sea was lit by moonlight. Now was the time to close for the kill but some more time was to elapse before he finally dived several miles ahead of the convoy in a position which, he had calculated, would be just right to attack the convoy. But he found to his dismay that he could barely make out the enemy ships through his periscope. The mist had thickened up once more. Suddenly as if from nowhere, the ships appeared out of the mist. He could clearly see a destroyer and the two merchantmen. With lightning skill, he made the series of calculations which gave him his firing angle for the torpedoes and a salvo of four was fired in a fan-like pattern, in the hope that he would catch both supply ships. By then the destroyer's bows were almost towering above the *Turbulent* and Linton quickly dived out of the way to avoid being rammed.

There came the awful wait until the first explosion came. One of the merchantmen was hit but then a curious sound reached the submariner's ears. It was the noise of a torpedo running wild. It had veered off course and was streaking around in circles. Seconds later there came another explosion as the second supply ship was hit. Then to Linton's delight came a third explosion a few moments later. The maverick torpedo had struck one of the destroyers.

The remaining serviceable destroyer plastered the area with depth charges but this attack had soon to halt because by then both merchantmen had gone to the bottom and the crippled destroyer was about to sink. The water was strewn with wreckage and survivors which the destroyer began to pick up.

Linton brought *Turbulent* to the surface shortly after dawn and was rewarded by the sight of only one destroyer. The other, the *Emmanivele Pessagno,* had gone to the bottom along with the two supply ships. Linton had avenged the terrible depth charging he had suffered in a most spectacular way during a patrol which the Captain (Submarines) at Alexandria described as '... the work of an astute and skilled artist'.[1]

The tribute paid him by the Captain (S) was no over-estimation of Linton's ability or piece of literary licence. Linton was an exacting professional whose technical skill was perhaps unmatched by other submarine commanders. But, as Jameson goes on to point out in his book,

> 'What he lacked was that inspired sixth sense by which some military commanders are able to guess the unforeseen. Linton, though technically almost perfect, extremely courageous and entirely competent was without this attribute of genius. Had he possessed it, he would not sometimes have been robbed of success by something which no one could have foreseen. "Unlucky" is the more general term.'

Linton was a powerhouse of energy, happy only when he was at sea and in action. The execution of his duty had almost taken on obsessional proportions for him. It is said that, on a visit to Malta to pick up fresh orders, 'Shrimp' Simpson asked him if

[1] From *Submariners V.C.* by Rear-Admiral Sir William Jameson, KBE, CB.

he would like to remain there for a few days' rest before continuing to sea. Linton turned down the offer pointing out that there were no targets to be had in Malta harbour! His visit to Malta lasted only four hours and he was off again.

Linton's score mounted as he carried out more and more patrols but it seemed that he was destined to be subjected to more depth charging than any other commander. During his sixth patrol in *Turbulent* Linton, who at the age of thirty-five was no youngster among submarine commanders, took another hammering when he was in the throes of attacking a convoy. He was spotted by escorting enemy aircraft which dropped markers and the subsequent depth charge attack did a great deal of minor damage to his boat, although this was later patched up, with the engineering expertise of his crew.

Linton, with fire in his belly, never let the opportunity of aggression pass him by. On his eighth patrol, the longest he was to undertake, he introduced some novel actions to relieve the boredom of finding no floating targets. He closed the shore and bombarded targets inland with his deck gun. This once almost left him high and dry for *Turbulent* grounded on some sunken wreckage and Linton had to extricate her by driving her off astern. In another inshore action, Linton forced an enemy ship to run aground, then he sent a torpedo into her, breaking her in half.

By the end of her first year in the Mediterranean, *Turbulent* had spent more than one-third of it on patrol and was due for a refit in England after two more patrols.

On her ninth patrol, Linton had *Turbulent* quickly in action when a convoy was sighted, heavily escorted by motor launches, destroyers and a squadron of aircraft. Linton sank a 10,000-ton supply ship before evading the depth charges that inevitably followed. No less than forty-eight hours later he sent another ship to the bottom with two torpedoes. Later, he sighted an oil tanker, under escort by destroyers, and this he sank after a protracted 'tail' had been kept on the convoy.

Over the following few days Linton sighted many worthy targets, but every time he attacked he was driven off by stiff opposition from escorts. Not to be outdone, he reverted to his bombarding technique and actually closed the shore and shelled a railway train which was standing in the station at St Ambroglio. From a range of over a mile, he scored many hits both on the train and the engine, a tribute to the skill of his gunners. But this attack roused the hornets' nest and soon fast Italian surface craft were speeding in on him and a nasty depth charge attack ensued during which some damage was sustained. But with his usual skill, Linton wriggled free of it to return to base and both the praise of his seniors and admiration of his comrades.

Towards the end of February 1943, *Turbulent* sailed on the patrol which was to be her last before making for England. It is known that she attacked and sank a ship off the coast of Boniacio then some days later, on 14 March, she was sighted off the Corsican coast. What happened to her after that is a mystery, for she was never seen again. She failed to reply to signals sent to her and after several days had elapsed following the date upon which she should have returned from patrol, the only conclusion possible could be drawn. *Turbulent* and Commander Linton were gone. What exactly happened to her no one knows for sure, but it is generally thought that she struck a mine off the north coast of Sardinia.

History had repeated itself. Linton, like Wanklyn, was lost on his last patrol. Linton had carried out his war in some of the most dangerous waters of all, with consummate skill and courage, sinking two warships and twenty-seven supply ships. During his period as a commander of *Pandora* and then *Turbulent* he had made more than twenty patrols and, in the space of less than two years, spent 460 days on patrol.

The loss of this tough and resilient commander came as a bitter blow to everyone of the First Flotilla. Apart from his success as a submariner he was also one of the Royal Navy's great characters and sadly missed by all who knew him. In May 1943 the greatness and skill of this valiant submariner was recognized, with the posthumous award of the Victoria Cross.

Yet another Naval officer was to crown himself in glory in these clear but dangerous waters and exact a considerable toll upon the enemy. He was Commander A. C. C. Miers, captain of the T-class submarine *Torbay*. Miers was an 'explosive' character in the full sense of the word; hot-tempered, precise and demanding of the highest standards both of his men *and* himself. He was aggressive both as a man and, what was more important, as a submarine commander; seizing every opportunity of striking at the enemy. He was utterly intolerant of inefficiency and ran a 'tight' and smoothly efficient ship where every single man aboard knew his job and carried it out with signal expertise under Miers' ever-watchful and critical eye.

Miers was a career sailor, the son of an army officer who was killed in one of the first actions of the First World War. He joined the Navy as a special entry cadet and volunteered for the Submarine Service in 1929. Seven years later, he was given his first command. When war came in 1939, Miers was obliged to spend several months in General Service, something he had been doing for two years previously, before he was finally appointed to command *Torbay*.

Throughout his naval career till that time, Miers had done little to endear himself to his fellow-officers. He was given to speaking his mind, irrespective of the consequences, and there were those who took exception to this. There was, however, little that could be done about it, for Miers was a gifted officer, meticulous in everything he did and a thorough stickler for efficiency. There were those among his fellows who predicted his downfall, but their predictions were to be proved utterly unfounded when Miers showed his mettle in the Mediterranean.

It is somewhat ironic that, for a man who was so greatly concerned with the paramount importance of his boat's efficiency, she set out on her way to the Mediterranean with an ill-trained crew. This was by no means Miers' doing. *Torbay* was at Portsmouth when urgent orders were received for every available submarine to put to sea and stand sentinel over the Bay of Biscay, where intelligence had prophesied that the German battle-cruisers *Scharnhorst* and *Gneisenau* were expected to make a dash into the German-held French port of Brest after being at large in the Atlantic. It was hoped that the submarines would be able to launch an attack on the battle-cruisers when they were steaming back into port. It transpired that almost half *Torbay*'s crew was on leave when the call to sea came and Miers had to recruit some young and mostly inexperienced crew to make up the boat's complement. The plan to ambush the two battle-cruisers proved abortive and *Torbay* was ordered to proceed to Gibraltar. Miers, ever the perfectionist, lost no time in working up his crew but, even under his exacting eye, this was inevitably to take time ... and there was little enough of that considering the situation that existed in the Mediterranean in the early months of 1941.

That the crew had not reached its optimum efficiency was reflected all too clearly during *Torbay*'s first patrol in the Mediterranean, when in April she attacked a convoy off Sardinia. The attack failed owing to a lack of co-ordination among the crew. Disheartened but determined to mould his crew into a proficient fighting unit, Miers went about training with a vengeance. After being sent to Alexandria to join the First Flotilla, and when he was ordered on his first patrol from his new station, *Torbay* went on that patrol with a crack crew – a hallmark of Miers' ability as a 'moulder' of men.

Any doubts about the efficiency of that crew were quickly dispelled when in broad daylight, and scorning the possibility of attack from the air, Miers surfaced and sank two small vessels by gunfire. Miers' next encounter exemplified the determination that was ingrained within him. He sighted an Italian tanker off Cape Helles but found to his consternation that the only position from which he could attack was at the tanker's stern. This he did and with remarkable skill he scored a hit on the rear of the enemy ship, bringing her to an abrupt halt. The tanker did not sink, however, but now, with her at a standstill, Miers manoeuvred round and fired another torpedo into her amidships, then headed off, content that the tanker would sink.

The tanker was, however, made of tougher stuff and when, the following day, he returned to the scene he found her still afloat. Reluctant to expend another torpedo, Miers put a scuttling party aboard; but their efforts to set light to the cargo of oil were thwarted and they had to abandon that idea. It when then that a Turkish ship arrived to take the tanker in tow. But Miers was determined that he wasn't going to have his prey whisked from under his nose so he fired another torpedo at her. This one, however, missed; but the sight of the torpedo was enough to put the Turkish boat to flight and Miers closed up his guns crew and began the mortal bombardment of the tanker which he left a blazing wreck, with a towering column of thick black smoke belching high into the sky for all to see.

Miers, not wanting to be around when the inevitable chase began, was on the point of departing the area when a lookout saw a convoy of several escorted ships coming his way. Miers' luck was in and he dived to manoeuvre into an attack position; but try as he might, his attempts were continuously frustrated by the zig-zagging of the convoy and the efforts of the destroyer escorts. However his luck held and he spotted a tanker, the 3,300-ton *Giuseppini Gherardi*, lagging behind the others. The opportunity was too good to miss and a clutch of torpedoes put paid to her.

Miers had notched up a good score on that second Mediterranean patrol and there were greater things to come. The third patrol proved even more fruitful when the Italian submarine *Janita*, together with a supply ship, seven small vessels and another tanker, fell to Miers' torpedoes and guns. There seemed to be no stopping the resolute and determined Miers and it was he who was selected for a special mission in which he was to land a party of commandos, led by Lieutenant Colonel Geoffrey Keyes, which was to carry out a raid on the headquarters of the German General Rommel in North Africa. The party of raiders was put ashore in extremely adverse conditions and, although the raid itself proved abortive because the building attacked was not in fact Rommel's headquarters, Colonel Keyes, a son of Admiral Sir Roger Keyes, who was killed in the action, was posthumously awarded the Victoria Cross.

In a similar operation off the island of Crete, Miers again showed the lengths to which he was prepared to go to ensure the success of an operation. He had on board a party of commandos to be landed on a beach by the use of folbots. When Miers surveyed the beach where the two parties of troops were to be landed, he found it was pounded incessantly by heavy waves, which would make it impossible for the troops to be landed safely. He therefore carried out a reconnaissance of the shoreline to find another spot where they could be landed with a greater chance of success. It is said that, in his determination to get a close look at the shore, he took his boat so near to the shore that he could clearly see the local peasants making their way to chapel! That night, having selected a suitable landing place, he surfaced; but the operation got off to a bad start when one of the folbots got damaged on the beach and the other badly holed when it bumped up against the casing of the submarine. Undaunted and determined to get the commandos ashore, he used a big rubber-made boat which he had captured from a German ship. The crew had nicknamed it 'Mauritania' but alas – this too sprang a leak and took some hours to mend before, finally, a few strong-armed men of *Torbay*'s crew rowed the soldiers ashore. Having successfully landed the army personnel, *Torbay* went in search of fodder for her torpedoes but Miers was unlucky and had to return to Alexandria.

Luck was to return to Miers on his next patrol which began on 20 February when he sailed out of Alexandria. The first five days of the patrol passed without notable event but as it progressed the weather worsened until on the night of the 26th it grew into a full-blown storm. That night Miers surfaced to recharge his batteries and the officers of the watch on the submarine's bridge caught the full force of the unrelenting storm. *Torbay* was off the island of Cephalonia and the torrential rains lashed the bridge, soaking everyone on it, in spite of their protective clothing. It was while this storm was at its height that a signal was received, informing Miers that an enemy tanker was heading in his direction.

The alert crew, tensed up with the prospect of engaging the enemy, waited as the storm became fickle, one minute raging then subsiding for a short while to allow the moon to shine down on the sea. It was during one of these bright patches that the lookouts saw the tanker steering a zig-zag course through the waves towards the submarine, with an escorting destroyer fussing protectively about ahead of her. Miers quickly summed up the situation and decided that his only hope of pulling off a successful attack would be to get astern of the tanker, out of the way of the destroyer escort. He took *Torbay* down and dived right under the tanker emerging at her stern on the surface, and wheeled around to launch his attack – but then the trouble began. The weather closed in again, making it well nigh impossible to get an accurate estimate of his target's speed and course. The progression along his course brought him in and out of torrential downpours of rain and at one critical point, he had to stop all engines because he had got so close to the tanker that he was almost on the point of collision. Finally he launched a torpedo but at the very moment that it left the tube, the heavy sea swept *Torbay*'s bows off course and the torpedo went wildly astray. Her track was, however, spotted, and the destroyer traced it and found *Torbay*. Immediately the escort charged towards the submarine and the ear-rending blast of the submarine's klaxon played the warning note to dive.

Miers, the last man off the bridge, was sliding down the ladder when *Torbay* began to sink beneath the waves but as he pulled the hatch over his head, it chose that moment to jam half open, allowing the water to sweep in. Miers did not bother to fight it, but left it and scrambled down through the lower hatch and slammed it shut. By then the conning tower was almost filled with water, making the task of catching a trim extremely difficult for the First Lieutenant. The difficulty was not helped either by the fact that the klaxon which had sounded the crash dive continued to blare, owing to a short circuit. This was soon remedied when the fuse was extracted but there came another more menacing noise as the destroyer loosed a pattern of depth charges which rocked the boat. Miers, however, managed to struggle clear of the onslaught. He was furious at missing such a promising target but his fury and rage reached its peak when he discovered what it was that was jamming the conning tower hatch – a pillow. Miers used this pillow to lean against when on watch. In the rush to get below when the crash dive came, the pillow had been forgotten.

Miers' bout of fury was not helped when on the two succeeding nights, *Torbay* came under severe depth charge attack after being caught napping on the surface by enemy destroyers. Indeed, so severe was the second attack that Miers rightly decided to 'move house' to another part of his billet, off the island of Corfu. He reached this area at dawn on 4 March and sighted an important convoy, comprising four troopships, with destroyer escorts and aircraft flying overhead. But to his fury the convoy out-paced him and he lost the chance of an attack. It soon began to disappear over the horizon. Fury tinged with bitter frustration charged Miers who was downright in his determination to reverse his bad fortune.

Hell-bent on catching a piece of the action, he studied the chart and it occurred to him strange that the convoy had hugged the coast so closely. To Miers this could mean but one thing – it was bound for the Corfu Roads, where it would anchor and refuel. He knew that this was often the pattern of events with Italian convoys. Nestling in the sanctuary of a well-defended harbour they could refuel and prepare themselves for the rest of their voyage. Miers resolved to attack the convoy while at anchor but this meant penetrating the stretch of sea between the island of Corfu and the Greek mainland, known as Corfu Harbour.

Miers was positioned off the south channel entry to the Harbour and his intention was beset with two major problems. First, he had no knowledge of the minefields that would inevitably bestride the Harbour and secondly, his batteries were running low. These he would first have to recharge before venturing into the Harbour; but time was against him. If he hesitated then he might well lose the chance of attacking the convoy for it was very likely that it would leave its anchorage the following morning. He therefore decided to enter the five-mile-long southern channel on the *surface*, timing his entry to coincide with the coming of darkness before moonrise. Then he planned to find himself a suitably secluded spot to hide and recharge his batteries before proceeding to the attack, which he hoped to carry out either during moonlight or at dawn.

When darkness came that night, Miers began the perilous journey through the south channel – a trip made doubly difficult by the fact that there was but a narrow stretch of water through which he could pass because of shoals reaching out from either shore; and he had to make the journey on the surface, using his electric motors to remain as silent as possible. Absolute quiet was observed aboard the boat but then came a stroke of luck. A lookout spotted a small vessel also penetrating the Harbour astern of *Torbay*. Miers put this craft to good use, for he dived and waited till it passed, then followed it up the channel, relying on its captain to know the way through the minefields. With the sound of the Italian craft's engine reverberating across the channel, Miers was able to bring one of his diesels into action and thereby recharge his batteries, partially at least.

Once in the Harbour, a patrol boat emerged out of the gloom and Miers had to dive quickly out of the way. Luckily he was not spotted and was able to surface again some time later when the coast was clear. By the time midnight had come and past, the batteries were almost fully recharged; more than enough to see them through the mission. Then at 1 a.m., another patrol vessel was sighted and Miers took *Torbay* under. This time, however, he was concerned as to whether or not the disturbance of the dive had aroused the suspicions of the Italians in the patrol boat and he lay dormant for a while before risking a look through the periscope. Half an hour later, the patrol boat made off.

Torbay, going ahead dead slow on just one motor, slipped across the Harbour for the following hour until at last, having dodged yet more patrol boats which it was clear had an inkling that there might be a submarine in the Harbour, he reached the Roads. Visibility was so poor, however, that he resigned himself to waiting until dawn before launching an attack. He backed out of the Roads to lie in wait for the dawn, but in doing so he almost rammed a darkened destroyer. Throughout the remainder of the night the patrol boats were active, listening and dropping small charges now and again that tested the nerves of the waiting submariners. Finally, after what seemed like an eternity, dawn came and Miers headed into the Roads to begin his attack. But as he nudged *Torbay* in she was almost rammed by a patrol boat and had to dive deep.

Again Miers brought *Torbay* on an attack course towards the Roads but by then it was broad daylight and the attack would be all the more dangerous; not to mention his escape back down the channel. When he finally reached the anchorage, he found to his utter disappointment that there were no troopships to be seen. It transpired that Miers had miscalculated the intentions of the troopship convoy. Instead of anchoring in the Roads, they had sailed straight on through the north channel and out into the open sea. But the anchorage was not bare. There were two supply ships lying peacefully at anchor and perfectly positioned for shots amidships. Nearby was a destroyer, not so well positioned, lying bow-on to the submarine. Miers loosed a salvo of six torpedoes, a cluster of two for each ship, then dived deep and headed back towards the south channel. As he did so the sound of violent explosions reached his ears. Two of the supply ships, one of 8,000 tons and another of 2,000 tons, were hit and sinking. The two torpedoes aimed at the destroyer had missed. Immediately the hornets' nest was roused but it was a sleepy crowd who launched themselves into the counter-attack. The attempt that was made to seek and destroy the intruder was both disorganized and ineffective. The Italians concentrated their search in the area from which the torpedoes had been fired which in itself was a gross miscalculation. It should have been fairly obvious, even to the half-awake defenders, that by now the submarine would be heading as fast as it could through either the north or south channels. As it was, by then *Torbay* was speeding south and Miers could hear the detonations of depth charges as they were dropped by a destroyer and patrol craft.

On her way south, charging away at periscope depth, *Torbay* passed patrol craft racing north. Just before mid-day, Miers reached the open sea, leaving chaos and bewilderment behind. By then the entire crew, some of whom, including Miers, had been on duty for upwards of twenty-four continuous hours, were utterly exhausted. Even so, it was not until that evening that *Torbay* could safely surface and recharge her batteries. As if her gallant foray into Corfu Harbour had not been enough, she received orders that night to extend her patrol by proceeding to the Gulf of Taranto, despite the fact that her patrol ought to have ended that day. She spent another thirteen days at sea before finally returning to Alexandria. During that extended patrol period, the thoroughly worn-out crew suffered from bouts of flu but Miers refused to bring his boat back until ordered to do so.

For that daring exploit, Miers was awarded the Victoria Cross, but it was awarded under somewhat unusual circumstances. Following her final patrol in the Mediterranean under Miers' command, during which she sank one minesweeper, a schooner, a merchantman and a petrol carrier, *Torbay* returned to England for a refit. Upon his return, Miers was summoned to Buckingham Palace to be invested with his award; but his entire crew had also been awarded various decorations and Miers insisted that they receive their decorations along with him – something which was in complete contravention of all the rules of protocol. The Lord Chamberlain would not hear of it but, typical of Miers, he made such a fuss that His Majesty the King intervened and so it was that when Miers received his Victoria Cross, he did so along with his officers and men. Typical of the man, he wanted to make absolutely sure that they got the same recognition as he.

The submariner served where the average sailor least wanted to be – beneath the waves. Indeed, the very construction of surface ships, together with the multitudinous array of safety equipment, lifeboats, life-jackets, etc., were all specifically designed to avoid what the submariner purposely did – that is venture below the surface. The very fact that these men *volunteered* to serve in what was basically a metal tube below the surface of the water in time of war, marks them in the eyes of most people (including the author) as extremely brave men. To go to war in such vessels makes them heroes to a man. We have seen, in the preceding chapters, men who have risen to the towering pinnacles of courage. The submariner claims that there is no greater danger in fighting in a submarine than there is in a surface warship – this claim is essentially born of modesty.

If ever a man's nerves were tested to the limit, it must have been during the time when he was subjected to depth charge attack. To withstand such an adventure and not 'crack' under the strain demands the ultimate in self-control. But there were other, perhaps even more dangerous occasions, like the one which is about to be re-told when the nervous tension of the moment is beyond belief. The incident in question concerns the submarine *Thrasher*, operating as part of the First Flotilla out of Alexandria....

Thrasher, under the command of Lieutenant H. S. Mackenzie, left the depot ship *Medway*, *en route* for its patrol area on Friday, 13 February 1942. There has long been a superstition among sailors that it is unlucky to sail on Friday the thirteenth. It was therefore with some trepidation that this patrol was embarked upon. The fears that sailing on such a day might be heightening the chances of disaster were to be fully justified.

The patrol got off to a bad start for, when *Thrasher* cruised towards her patrol area off Crete, she sighted a convoy before dawn on the 16th but the darkness of the night foiled Mackenzie's attempts to attack and the convoy slipped into the sanctuary of harbour before Mackenzie could try again. Daybreak brought with it bright sunshine, clear skies and a placid sea, about the worst possible combination of weather a submarine could wish for. In the clear waters of the Mediterranean, a submarine could easily be spotted from the air while at periscope depth, particularly in a calm sea. Mackenzie was concerned that he might have been detected during his abortive attempt to attack the convoy and his fears were realized when later that morning a succession of patrol craft swept out of Suda Bay and carried out short 'sweeps' of the area. Later came an anti-submarine craft which carried out a listening sweep, obviously searching for *Thrasher*; but Mackenzie's skill evaded detection and she slipped away from the scene. It was not long after that lookouts spotted the tell-tale wisp of smoke on the horizon that betrayed the presence of a ship. Binoculars swept the sea and the sky and sure enough there above it was an aircraft. This could mean but one thing – a convoy under escort. Mackenzie soon saw the wisp of smoke materialize into a merchant ship, deeply laden with cargo and heavily escorted by five anti-submarine boats, forming a ring around her. Above the ship was the aircraft, with its crew intent on the sea below, ever watchful for the lurking submarine. Then a second aircraft appeared. The Italians obviously placed great importance upon this ship, which made it, from Mackenzie's point of view, all the more valuable as a target.

Mackenzie set course to close the convoy but taking the precaution of only quick looks through the periscope to check speed, bearing and course then running deep to avoid detection by the aircraft as the two enemies closed. *Thrasher*'s seamen were at their stations, ready for the opportunity to fire. The target was a difficult one. Mackenzie could chance only brief glimpses through the periscope lest he should give away his position and on one such look he found himself almost on the point of being rammed by a patrol boat. He managed to dive clear but when he again got up to periscope depth he found himself in an awkward firing position abaft the beam of the merchant ship. Mackenzie fired a salvo of four torpedoes but he had no sooner done so than there were two explosions danger-ously close to *Thrasher*. These were not the sounds of explosion from torpedoes but of bombs. *Thrasher* rocked when the ex-plosions occurred but it appeared that no damage had been done and Mackenzie took her deep. Then came the satisfactory thuds of two torpedoes striking home on their target.

No sooner had the muffled explosions of the torpedoes died away than the submarine's Asdic operator reported that no fewer than three of the patrolling Italian craft had caught *Thrasher* in their sonar beams and were closing in for the kill. Thirty depth charges were dropped in a bid to secure *Thrasher*'s fate but although some of them came dangerously close to doing so, none of them succeeded and it was with great relief that the attack subsided and the Italians were heard to move off.

When Mackenzie brought *Thrasher* to periscope depth and had a look, he found to his satisfaction a sinking merchant ship, with the craft which had hunted him still attempting to find him, but now in a different area. Content that for the time at least, he was safe, he took *Thrasher* deep to reload his tubes. When he subsequently brought the submarine to the surface the sea was bare of ships. They were alone and thankfully able to have a well-earned respite. As everyone except the lookouts enjoyed the inrush of fresh air and a period of rest, Mackenzie reflected upon the events of the past few hours, particularly the hazardously narrow escape they had had from the aircraft's bombs. *Thrasher* got under way, slipping through the stretch of sea between Crete and the Greek mainland and out into the open sea where she was met by a heavy sea, which she ploughed through. Her lookouts stayed ever watchful lest she be caught unawares by enemy patrol boats but none came in sight. Then she altered course, but in doing so, this brought her beam on to the swell of the sea and she began to roll quite violently.

It was Petty Officer Gould, the second coxswain who, while off duty, first heard it – an unusual thudding noise every time *Thrasher* rolled, just as if something were loose. Others too heard this strange noise and as one of the ratings passed close underneath the gun tower, he heard a strange clicking sound. It appeared that something was loose in the casing near the deck gun. The seaman who was going on watch reported what he had heard to the captain and Mackenzie sent a seaman down on to the casing to investigate. When he got there he found to his horror that there was a gaping hole in the casing, just beneath the revolving gun platform. Making all haste in spite of the heavy sea, the seaman scrambled back to the bridge where he reported his find to Mackenzie.

The captain selected his First Lieutenant, Lieutenant Roberts, and the second coxswain, Petty Officer Gould, to go and investigate the gaping hole. It had already occurred to Mackenzie that it might have been as a result of the air attack they had suffered earlier. Roberts and Gould made their way to the gun platform and found a live bomb lying on the deck just in front of the gun shield. It was some three feet long and a little more than six inches in diameter. The sight of the bomb was menacing in itself but even more so were the damaged fins. Both men realized that with the bomb being damaged there was a fair chance that it might well explode at any moment – this was no dud. The rolling motion of the submarine could, they quickly surmised, cause the bomb to roll off the deck and on to the casing where it might well explode and blow them and the submarine to kingdom come. Gould grabbed the bomb in a bid to keep it steady while Roberts moved back along the deck with all haste to report to Mackenzie.

Mackenzie, once in the picture, ordered an alteration in course which brought the submarine stern on to the swell which stopped the rolling and lessened the chances of the bomb slipping off the deck. A sack was called for and, grabbing it, Roberts scrambled back along the slim deck to where Gould was still clutching the bomb. Then came the tricky part. The bomb was not unduly heavy and they succeeded in edging it into the sack but they still had the problem of making their way along the very narrow slippery deck to the bows, some 100 feet away, where they could toss it into the sea. One false move, one tiny slip on their journey, would send the bomb tumbling down on to the bulging pressure hull or saddle tanks of *Thrasher* and it would explode.

A rope was tied around the sack to enable the two men to handle it more easily and they began their trek along the narrow deck, cautiously judging every step they took. Gingerly they made their way along it until they finally came to a 'bump' in the deck at the extreme forward end of it – this was a feature of this type of submarine and both men had to negotiate this slippery incline before they could reach the bows proper. To make matters worse this was the slimmest part of the deck and even greater care had to be taken in sidling along. At last they reached the point where they were clear of the main casing and saddle tanks. Gently they lowered the bomb over the side until it was a scant few inches above the water's surface. Then Mackenzie ordered half astern. The boat jolted backwards and the bomb was gone ... much to the relief of the crew and in particular the gallant duo who had disposed of it. Still, however, they were not quite out of the woods for they reasoned that the bomb was probably fitted with a hydrostatic detonating device and they had to retreat with all speed.

No explosion followed but there was still something puzzling the two men. The bomb they had found had been in *front* of the gun platform but the gaping hole was underneath it. How then could the bomb have been where it was found if there was a hole? A further investigation had to be carried out and it was then that the horrible truth was discovered – there was yet another bomb, wedged between the pressure hull and the circular trunk which supported the four-inch gun, in the gap between the casing and the pressure hull. It would have been difficult to find a more awkward place for a bomb to get itself wedged.

To understand just how tricky an operation the extraction of the bomb was to be it is necessary to know a little about the submarine's construction. The pressure hull itself is long and cylindrical, rather like a cigar. It is inside this hull that the whole operation of the submarine takes place. Outside this 'dry' hull are the saddle tanks. These are bulbous ballast tanks used in the diving and surface operation of the submarine. Running from stem to stern of the boat is a narrow deck along which the crew can walk. The deck comprises a continuous platform, perforated with many hundreds of holes through which water can enter or leave as the boat surfaces or dives. This platform is raised about three to four feet from the pressure hull and contains a complex of pipes and a stowage place for ropes, etc. It was in this gap just by the gun platform support that the bomb was lodged.

On the deck there is a series of gratings which allow entry to stowage compartments while the boat is either on the surface or in harbour. The problem facing the two 'bomb-disposal men', Roberts and Gould, was that the nearest of these hatches through which the bomb could be got out was some twenty feet from where it was lodged and there was only enough room in the restricted gap for a man to crawl or slide along its length. Furthermore, with the submarine on the surface in enemy waters, there was a fair chance that she might have to dive if threatened with air attack. If the men were in the gap at that time they would certainly drown as the water gushed in through the small holes in the deck.

To get to the bomb the two men would have to wriggle along this gap in complete darkness, unstick the bomb and bring it back to the hatch; then adopt the same procedure as before by wrapping it in a sack and throwing it over the bows. Roberts and Gould both wriggled along the clearance between the deck and the pressure hull until at last they reached the bomb. Viewing it by the light of a torch they discovered that it was not wedged, as they had first thought, but rolling free – inside the gun support which it had penetrated as well as the casing. Luckily the bomb had not apparently been damaged and the prong-like detonating 'fingers' at the tip of the bomb were still intact. But this was not to say that it was not a delayed action bomb which might explode at any moment. They could not pull the bomb back out through the hole which it had made and out on to the deck because of the ragged edges of the hole, so it meant negotiating it back along the 'tunnel' to the grating.

Both men got a firm grip on the bomb and it came free quite easily; but as it did so their hearts almost stopped for it gave an ominous clicking sound which, to two men who had no knowledge of the workings of bombs, instinctively meant that the firing mechanism was operating. For a few seconds they waited but nothing happened and they proceeded on their way. But then they came to a point where the gap was so shallow that it meant lying flat and pulling and pushing the bomb along in a sled-like action with Gould holding the bomb in his arms while Roberts pulled him along. At last, however, they reached the hatch, having lost the torch which gave them a tiny speck of light by which to work. In complete darkness they finished the job by reaching the grating.

These few words of description may seem to give the impression that their task was fairly straightforward; but when one considers that the passage from the gun platform to the grating took forty minutes, then the immense nervous and physical strain under which the two men must have been becomes obvious. Nothing could have been more wonderful to the two men than the sight of the square of moonlight coming through the grating and the sound of Lieutenant Fitzgerald's voice as he bent over it and helped them out. Again the process of carrying it along the casing to the bows and dropping it into the water was carried out but not before the bold mariners had taken time out to examine the bomb which had caused them so much trouble and noted the various markings on it! Then, and only then, did it follow its partner into the sea. The entire operation of disposing of the two bombs had taken Roberts and Gould almost two tension-filled hours. After such a hair-raising experience, Mackenzie might well have been justified in abandoning the patrol and returning to base – but not he. *Thrasher* continued on her patrol and completed it although luckily there was no repetition of the excitement.

Four months after that terrifying experience, Lieutenant Peter Roberts and Petty Officer Thomas Gould were each invested with the Victoria Cross, a richly deserved reward for an act of supreme courage.

The accounts of heroism enacted in the Mediterranean and related here are but a few among many. Men like Tompkinson, in *Urge*, who accounted for the severe damaging of two Italian battleships as well as many other ships; Bryant, in *Safari*, the commander who had suffered so terribly at the hands of Germans' depth charges in the Skagerrak, notched up a formidable score, even though he arrived towards the end of the Mediterranean campaign; Caley, in *Utmost*, created havoc among enemy shipping but was lost when he took command of another submarine – these and many more made an indelible mark on the British submarine campaign in the Mediterranean.

But with the coming of 1943 and the subsequent Italian surrender, the campaign was all but over. Between June 1940, when Italy entered the war, and the end of 1944, British submarines and Allied submarines working under British control, sank 286 ships, totalling 1,030,960 tons.[1] This does not include many small ships under 500 tons which were sent to the bottom. The effect of such losses unquestionably played a large part in the downfall of the Axis forces fighting in North Africa and the ultimate successful invasion of Italy. Among the submarine successes were four cruisers, nine destroyers, eight torpedo boats and a corvette, as well as sixteen Italian and five German submarines.

These successes – so crippling to the enemy – were, however, not achieved without serious loss to the Royal Navy. Forty-five of her own submarines, not to mention seven other Allied submarines which were lost on patrol, one of them an Italian which had joined forces with the British after her country's surrender.

When one considers the grossly inadequate surface naval strength available when Italy entered the war, the part played by the British submarines was absolutely critical and helped to bring about the successful conclusion of the North African Campaign.

There was yet another theatre of war, in hotter climes, where the British submariner was called to fight an infinitely more terrible foe – the Japanese, in the Far East. Owing to the withdrawal of all British submarines from the Far East station upon the outset of the war in Europe there was, when Japan entered the war in December 1941, not a single British submarine in Far Eastern waters – and this situation was to exist for some time before a sizeable force could be built up.

When the Mediterranean war came in 1940, there was an urgent need for submarines in that theatre and every available British boat was withdrawn from the Far East to reinforce the sadly depleted Mediterranean flotillas. This left the two principal Far East stations, Hong Kong and Singapore, with no submarines and a mere handful of surface ships with which to counter any offensive by Germany's ally, Japan.

Britain realized that, in the event of war with Japan, resistance would be minimal and totally ineffective without the active support of other nations with colonies in that part of the world. The Dutch seemed the most likely to come to the aid of the British and indeed it was they who, by agreement, seconded

[1] From *The war at sea*, by Captain S. W. Roskill, DSC, RC.

a group of submarines to the British commander-in-chief. The Dutch, then, took part in the first submarine actions on behalf of the British in that area, when early in December, two of them took part in operations out of Singapore. They were K-17 and O-16. Then on 10 December those same two, in concert with three others, K-11, K-12 and K-13 took up patrol lines off the coast of Thailand. The day following the beginning of their patrols, two more Dutch submarines joined up with the British force, O-19 and O-20, when they set sail from their base to Singapore.

The plan was to set up Singapore as the main naval base for the Far East but as will be seen events were to completely change that strategy. The commanders of the Dutch boats were as daring as one could find and in the opening weeks they went about their offensive with a vengeance. The submarine O-16 achieved spectacular victories when, during a night attack while on the surface off the Kra Isthmus, Bussemaker, her commander, sank no fewer than four supply ships carrying troops – and this he achieved in waters where he knew he could not dive for they were so shallow. For this action, he was admitted to the DSO.

The Japanese Navy virtually ruled the seas in the Far East and with such a pitifully small group of Allied submarines there was little that could be done to stem the increasing tide of supply and warships plying the oceans, ferrying troops, ammunition, guns and other vital supplies to feed the army that would soon swarm through Malaya and cause the ultimate downfall of Singapore. The Dutch boats, their commanders, and crews fought valiantly but they were fighting a losing battle against a seemingly omnipotent foe.

A series of setbacks did nothing to instil any hope that things might improve. Both O-16 and O-20 were sunk and K-13 suffered an explosion, killing some of her crew and putting her out of action. To add further salt to the wound, the United States – who promised that, in the event of a Japanese war, she would reinforce the Singapore base with sixteen submarines – now had a change of heart and decided to send them to Australia instead. This was a loss that the British Eastern Fleet could ill-afford, particularly since the American submarines had minelaying capabilities and an adequate supply of mines, which could have taken a serious toll of Japanese shipping.

There was, however, one glimmer of hope on an otherwise

dark horizon, the British submarines *Trusty* and *Truant*, respectively under the command of Lieutenant Commander King and Lieutenant Commander Haggard, were ordered to join the Far East Fleet, together with another Dutch submarine. But before they arrived the existing submarines were to be engaged in action in which they were to achieve notable successes.

The Japanese sent a large invasion force to Borneo and Sarawak. Every available submarine was to put to sea to halt the invasion forces. Two submarines in particular distinguished themselves. K-14 sank no fewer than three transports and a tanker in convoy while K-16 accounted for a destroyer. Alas these successes were marred by the loss of two other Dutch submarines and the knowledge that, however hard they had tried and however valiantly they had fought, the submarines failed to stem the tide of the Japanese advance. Sheer weight of numbers set against a tiny handful of submarines proved just too much for them.

The situation in Singapore at the turn of the year was decidedly 'hot', for Japanese air raids were making it well nigh impossible to operate effectively as a submarine base. The result was that the submarines had to be withdrawn, the Dutch taking theirs to one of their own bases but still remaining under British command.

Trusty, on arrival in the Far East, went straight into the thick of the fighting. After a short stop at Singapore, she went to the China Sea and the Gulf of Siam where she found an abundance of small but important targets, carrying a wide variety of supplies. Most of these she was able to sink with her deck gun. Alas, this run of fortune was not to last for long. During her brief stay at Singapore she had sustained some damage and unbeknown to her commander, *Trusty* was in need of major refit owing to her having grounded on the passage out to the Far East. It was only when she put into Sourabaya, the Dutch base, that this was discovered and she was ordered to make for Colombo, in Ceylon, to undergo repairs.

Truant on the other hand did not enjoy the initial burst of success which attended *Trusty*. Haggard, avoiding Singapore when he arrived in the Far East, made for the Dutch base where he was ordered to patrol off Bali. Although he found an abundance of enemy ships there, he was also subjected to severe anti-submarine activity in the shape of highly competent Japanese patrols. On one occasion, Haggard sighted a Jap cruiser shepherding a convoy and prepared to attack. Time and again he was warded off by concentrated anti-submarine activity but at last he fired a salvo of six torpedoes at the cruiser – not one of which obliged him by exploding on target. Fewer things could have been more frustrating for a submarine commander than to have been subjected to severe attack, to have squirmed out of it, got the target in sight then have his attempts foiled by faulty torpedoes. Furthermore, after the abortive attack, *Truant* was once more subjected to fierce depth charge attack. To add further frustration to his patrol, Haggard had to temper his enthusiasm for the fray with caution for, although he sighted several submarines during the remainder of the patrol, he dared not shoot for fear that they might be Americans. He had been warned of the possibility that American submarines may have strayed into that area.

By then the Japanese had swarmed down the Malay Peninsula and Singapore fell on 15 February. The Dutch base at Sourabaya had not the proper facilities to cope with the repairs required by *Truant* so she too had to make for Ceylon which, because of the rapid Japanese advance, was becoming the focal point of Naval activity and the centre for operations. There was a strong possibility that the island of Ceylon would soon become a target for a Japanese invasion and both *Truant* and *Trusty*, soon back in full service again, were given the task of standing sentinel over the Malacca Straits, the obvious route through which an invasion force would come. This at least, it was hoped, would give some prior warning of an impending invasion. Unfortunately, only one of the two British submarines could operate in the area at a time and this was grossly inadequate for the task. The Dutch could offer no help either for their boats and crews had long since reached the point of total exhaustion.

Fears that an invasion attempt upon Ceylon and southern India was imminent were reinforced by a lightning aerial bombardment of the island by Japanese bombers. In spite of the intensity of the attack, however, no appreciable damage was done, and none worth mentioning was suffered by the submarine contingent on the island. With the ever-increasing possibility of a full-scale Japanese attempt to rout the British from that part of the world and so deny them a valuable naval base, the importance of some forewarning was critical. This could be done only by the positioning of submarines at strategic points along the anticipated route of an invading force. All possible haste had to be applied to the reinforcement of the submarines in Ceylon, together with the installation and establishment of a permanent and properly equipped base for the submarines.

As the year drew on and *Trusty* and *Truant* carried out patrols, it became necessary for both of them to have major dockyard overhauls, something which could not be undertaken anywhere other than in England; so they were both ordered home. This left the Far East Fleet with the remnants of the Dutch submarines to keep up the watch on the Malacca Straits and forewarn of an invading force's approach. The upshot of this was that there was no longer a single British submarine in the Far East, where to say the least the war was hotting up at an alarming pace.

In fact it was not until July of 1943 that eight ocean-going submarines were finally ordered to be detached from the Mediterranean Fleet and sent to the Far East. They were *Tally Ho*, *Templar*, *Tactician*, *Trespasser*, *Taurus*, *Severn*, *Surf* and *Simoon*. The last of these boats was, alas, never to see her new station for she was sunk in the Aegean before she could leave. Her place was taken by *Trident* which made for the Far East and upon arrival there lost no time in going straight on patrol. During this patrol she sighted, but was unable to attack, a Japanese cruiser, the *Kashi*, near Sabang in Sumatra. It was clear that there would be rich pickings for the submarines in that area and Their Lordships decided to allot even more submarines which were under construction for that area.

With the sudden arrival of so many submarines, it was crucial that a really first-class depot ship should be available to them and so it was that the depot ship *Adamant* was based on Trincomalee, in Ceylon.

Lieutenant Wingfield, in the submarine *Taurus*, was the first of the 'new boys' to draw blood on any appreciable scale when on 12 November he sighted and sank the Japanese submarine I-34 as it made its way into the approaches to Penang, Malaya. Cheering as this success was, it was not enough and it was not until the following year that the British submarines based on Trincomalee really began to bite – and they did it with lethal venom.

The Malacca Straits was the scene of most of the operations, the slim stretch of water between Sumatra and Malaya, where so much Japanese traffic sailed. One of the first to earn his spurs in that region was Commander Bennington, in *Tally Ho*, whose torpedoes accounted for the 5,100-ton Japanese cruiser *Kuma*. She immediately came under bitter counter-attack from escorts but the crafty Bennington foxed his hunters by heading for the shore rather than out to sea where he was expected to run and in so doing was able to slip away undamaged. He was not to get off lightly though for later he was attacked by a Japanese torpedo boat while on the surface. The Jap tried to ram him but failed on the first run. His second run was more successful, however, and he ripped open one of the *Tally Ho*'s ballast tanks. Luckily, the Jap was also severely damaged and in no position to continue the attack so Bennington was able to escape.

Bennington got back to Ceylon where repairs were carried out and he put to sea again in search of fresh fodder, which he found in the shape of the German submarine (formerly Italian) U-It.23. *Tally Ho*'s torpedoes sent her to the bottom.

Bennington was not the only commander to reap rewards. Lieutenant Beckley, in *Tempar*, caught the 7,000-ton cruiser *Kitigami* off Penang on 26 January and severely damaged her, although not enough to sink her.

Much to the consternation of submarine commanders there appeared a shortage of sizeable merchantmen to attack and successes were comparatively few. In general, they were the smaller coastal type of ship which were, because of the shallow waters in which they sailed, difficult targets for the submarines to engage. In the first five months of the year eight merchant ships of over 500 tons were sunk, making a total of 16,000 tons – not a particularly outstanding success rate.

In achieving that small but nevertheless important score, there were moments of excitement tinged on one occasion with hilarity. During the first patrol, Lieutenant Verschoyle-Campbell, in *Stonehenge*, came under severe depth charge attack. So terrifying was the attack that, quite by accident, a torpedo-man manning a stern tube fired off a torpedo which by some fluke actually hit and sank one of the surface attackers, a minesweeper. *Stonehenge* was later to notch up another success when she sank the 1,000-ton auxiliary *Choko Maru* but soon afterwards she was lost, the only submarine casualty suffered during that period. There were, however, many casualties among the submariners themselves, but these were of a different nature. The temperature aboard the submarines in the Far East often reached the 120-degree mark and whole crews would suffer the agonies of prickly heat or worse still heat stroke. These symptoms, coupled with the ever-present tension, heightened the uncomfortable conditions under which submariners operated in these climates.

The operations carried out by HM submarines working out of Trincomalee were many and varied and included 'cloak-and-dagger' missions, landing agents or sabotage teams on enemy-held coasts. These operations were often as dangerous for the submarines as they were for the men who went ashore, lying as they were in shallow water waiting for the return of their 'party', ever-watchful lest a Japanese patrol boat should catch them unawares.

Since most of the attacks carried out by our submarines were against small junks, carrying ammunition, petrol, rubber and other vital supplies, these were invariably sunk by gunfire. This, of course, necessitated the carrying of extra ammunition on board the submarine and as Commander Lipscomb points out in his book, *The British Submarine,*

'... matters got to such a pitch that submarines sailed with gun ammunition stowed in every possible place, including under the wardroom table! ... The story goes that rounds stowed behind the engines caused most anxiety but all survived and killed many Japanese'.

Lieutenant Commander Edward Young, RNVR, commanding *Storm* (incidentally the first RNVR officer to command a submarine) was a master at the art of using his gun and went 'poaching' in enemy held harbours in Burma where he wrought havoc among the small ships anchored there.[1]

Submarines patrolling the Malacca Straits also found themselves doing the work of the air/sea rescue service, picking up Allied airmen shot down while attacking targets in Sumatra. Going 'down in the drink' in these waters was singularly hazardous because of the ever-present threat of sharks. Many Allied airmen had good cause to be thankful to the Submarine Service for their timely arrival.

Commander William King in *Telemachus* added another

[1] Young gives a graphic account of his submarine's actions in that part of the world in his book *One of our submarines*, published by Rupert Hart-Davis, in 1953.

Japanese submarine to the scoreboard when he caught the I-166 off Penang and sent her to the bottom. Two months later *Trenchant*, under the command of Lieutenant Commander Hezlet, accounted for another submarine, this time a German, the U-859, and the hat-trick was completed when the Dutch submarine *Zwaardvisch* sank the German submarine U-168 near Java on 5 October. She quickly followed this up by sinking the Japanese minelayer *Itsukashima*. It was Hezlet in *Trenchant* who also fulfilled another of the varied tasks allotted to the submarines when he took two chariots (human torpedoes) to Phuket Harbour where they succeeded in destroying a 5,000-ton supply ship and severely damaging another.

During the latter period of 1944, British submarines were responsible for the sinking of more than 35,500 tons of enemy shipping which comprised sixteen merchant ships of over 500 tons.

Their greatest problem was actually finding enemy targets. The submariners of the Far East Fleet were not graced with the good fortune which attended their comrades in the Mediterranean theatre – at least not at that time. Furthermore their boats were far from adequate for the job. Captain Roskill, the official historian, sums up the situation. He says in *The war at sea*:

'Their work was all the more commendable because the "S" and "T" class boats were by no means suited to long patrols in tropical waters; their base facilities – on which submarines must always greatly rely for rest and refitting – had until 1944 been grossly inadequate; and the waters in which they had to work were often both difficult and dangerous.'

With the coming of 1945, the principal objectives in the sea war in the Far East were all too clear. By then there were two quite separate fleets operating in that area, the British Pacific Fleet which operated under the command of the Americans and the other the Eastern Fleet. The latter's objective was to deny the Japanese the use of the Indian Ocean and strangle her supply line to her forces on land, i.e. through the Malacca Straits. Moreover, the submarines and surface ships were to act in close support of the land forces of the British and Commonwealth armies. Despite these objectives, targets of any substantial size were still hard to find, especially for the Eastern Fleet. But there were a few and although most of them were attacked by gunfire, there were still a few opportunities to fall back on the torpedo.

There occurred at the turn of the year one of the all-time epics of sea chase when the British submarine *Shakespear*, under the command of Lieutenant Swanston, took it upon herself to attack a convoy steaming by the Andaman Islands. Swanston sank a 2,500-ton merchantman on New Year's Eve and three days later sighted a 700-ton merchantman for the attention of his torpedoes but alas, his aim was off and all of them missed. Furious at missing, he brought *Shakespear* to the surface and engaged the enemy with his deck gun, whereupon the merchantman returned the fire, but by then Swanston had scored a couple of hits. It was then that someone on the bridge sighted what was taken to be a submarine chaser bearing down on them. At that very moment, the guns crew on the Japanese merchantman found their mark and a shell slammed into the submarine, passing through the pressure hull, and water started to flood in. The submarine was on its way down, the diving order already having been given, and her progress down was arrested just in time. Immediately the guns crew closed up once more and engaged the merchantman, this time knocking out her gun with accurately directed fire.

Summoning all the engine power he could muster, Swanston took *Shakespear* out of range of the submarine chaser; but throughout the remainder of the day, Japanese aircraft launched continuous attacks on the crippled boat, which had to make a dash for home on the surface. No fewer than twenty-five separate air attacks were made on the submarine by Japanese bombers, fighters, seaplanes and fighter-bombers. In spite of the ferocity of the attacks, during which *Shakespear* sustained even greater damage, her gunners shot down one Jap aircraft and damaged four others. The end of the day brought a merciful respite from the aerial attacks and although the Japanese did not return, it was to take a further two days until finally *Shakespear* was taken in tow by another submarine and brought back to base.

For the British submarines operating out of Trincomalee, the targets offered were invariably small and it was to their comrades operating out of Freemantle that the possibilities of catching the really big fish fell. But if these giants were denied them the boats from Trincomalee did valiant work among the smaller fry and more than compensated for the lack of big prizes. They brought hell and damnation down upon anything Japanese that moved in the Malacca Straits and they did not reserve their attentions exclusively for targets at sea. Whenever the opportunity presented itself, the submarine commanders would close the shore, bombarding anything that looked like a worthy target – railways, trains, fuel dumps, enemy transports. It was not unknown, and indeed became quite commonplace, for a demolition party to be put ashore to blow up piers or similar installations on shore then retreat back to the submarine. The ingenuity and determination of the submariners knew no bounds – if targets did not present themselves, then they would go out and find them.

Submarines out of Trincomalee played a brilliant part in reconnaissance, sighting enemy warships and, if an attack were not possible, warning the British surface fleet to engage them. One such sighting made by *Statesman* and *Subtle* in May 1945, resulted in the 10,000-ton cruiser *Naguro* being sunk by surface forces, along with an attendant destroyer.

Commander Hezlet chalked up a notable success when he left Freemantle on patrol, having been posted there with other boats from Trincomalee, and torpedoed the 10,000-ton Japanese cruiser *Ashigara*, off Sumatra. Operating in very shallow waters and having negotiated an Allied minefield, Hezlet fired eight torpedoes at the cruiser and five of them found their mark. The cruiser was blasted apart and sank within minutes. *Trenchant* later scored another success in August when she sank the Jap minesweeper '105'.

By now, however, the war was about to come to an end but the British submarines fought on right up to the very end. *Stubborn*, commanded by Lieutenant Davies, in a brilliant and extremely difficult attack, torpedoed and sank a 750-ton destroyer. Two other submarines, *Tiptoe* and *Trump*, each claimed a victory; when working together they attacked a convoy and sank one 6,000-ton ship and another 4,000-ton ship.

These were among the last of the British submarine successes in the Far East where during the operational period there they had sunk no less than 97,000 tons of Japanese merchant shipping and damaged almost 15,000 tons as well as accounting for a further twelve merchant ships which were sunk by mines laid by submarines.

The war in Europe had long been over by the time the atomic bombs which finally brought Japan to her knees were dropped. British submarines had fought a brave war, carrying out their most successful patrols in the Mediterranean, but this had not been achieved without considerable loss of fine boats and gallant crews. Ninety British or Commonwealth submarines were lost in the entirety of the war – a high price to pay for victory. Of these, more than half were lost in the theatre where the British submarine had its finest hour of glory – the Mediterranean. British submarines never did achieve the momentous scores which attended the enemy submarines, but this was for the sole reason that the enemy ships were just not there to sink, and in no way reflected upon the outstanding ability of her submariners.

Midget Submarines

The battleship *Tirpitz* was one of the largest and most powerful warships built for the German Navy during the Second World War. In her lifetime, she left Germany's shores only once, never to return. On that one and only foray away from home shores, she spent most of her time in the sanctuary of heavily defended anchorages in Norwegian fjords and yet in spite of the seemingly passive role determined for her by the German Naval High Command, she posed for a period the greatest possible threat to Britain's survival of the war.

Winston Churchill was keenly aware of the potential menace of *Tirpitz*. In January 1942, news reached him that *Tirpitz* lay at anchor at Trondhejm, deep in a Norwegian fjord. He wrote:

'The presence of *Tirpitz* at Trondhejm has now been known for three days. The destruction or even the crippling of this ship is the greatest event at sea in the present time ... no other target is comparable to it. ... The entire naval situation throughout the world would be altered. ... The whole strategy of the war turns at this period on this ship, which is holding four times the number of British ships paralysed, to say nothing of the two new American battleships retained in the Atlantic. I regard the matter as of the highest urgency and importance.'

Churchill's estimation of the situation was correct. *Tirpitz* posed a considerable threat to Arctic convoys and her destruction was of crucial importance to the war effort. The Royal Air Force acted swiftly.

While she remained at Trondhejm, *Tirpitz* was just within

range of the RAF's heavy bombers. No fewer than five bombing missions were carried out during her four-month stay in the fjord. Fourteen aircraft were lost and not a single bomb hit *Tirpitz*. The might of anti-aircraft fire power from shore batteries was such that the task of driving home an aerial attack was hopeless. Even if they had succeeded in striking the giant ship, it is doubtful if the bombs the RAF was using at that time would have made much impression upon her heavily armoured hull.

Over the months that followed while *Tirpitz* remained in Norwegian waters, moving from one safe anchorage to another and in so doing mobilizing the British Home Fleet, repeated attempts were made to deal her a crushing blow, but none of them succeeded. It was to be more than a year later that events turned in favour of the Royal Navy and the first devastating blow was struck at this floating behemoth, the wound that was lead to her final destruction.

Determined RAF and Fleet Air Arm attacks had failed to make any impression upon *Tirpitz* and the cost of these strikes in men and machines was mounting alarmingly. In October 1942, a cunningly conceived human-torpedo attack on the battleship while she lay at anchor in Fottenfjord ended in disaster for the attackers. It seemed that *Tirpitz* was invincible, but there were those who for some time had been planning and scheming to hit her in a revolutionary and dramatic way.

Early in September 1943, *Tirpitz* slipped into Altenfjord in the far north of Norway, within the Arctic Circle. This vast fjord, screened from the sea by the islands of Söröy, Seiland and Stjernöy, cut deep into the land. Its placid waters were skirted by towering mountains, snow-covered for much of the year. There could not have been a more ideal haven for the *Tirpitz*. A minefield extended across the main access route to the fjord. But the pride of the German Navy had even more intensive protection when she reached the anchorage in Kaa Fjord, a smaller almost landlocked fjord at the end of the major canyon of water. Around her were shore batteries, anti-submarine nets and sonar detection devices for tracing intruder submarines, as well as Luftwaffe aircraft which kept an almost constant surveillance over the fjord. A mighty steel mesh anti-submarine net sealed the mouth of Kaa Fjord where *Tirpitz* dropped anchor near the shore.

Around *Tirpitz* lay three layers of anti-torpedo nets fashioned out of nine-inch interlocking steel grommets and able to withstand an attack by the most powerful torpedoes of the day. The outer torpedo net hung directly from the water's surface while a middle one was suspended on long steel wire attached to buoys. The final and inner net was anchored to the sea-bed, making a seemingly impenetrable shield against underwater torpedo attack. Close to the shore was the only entrance to this netted refuge.

Held fast to the shore by mooring wires, both her anchors lay on the fjord's bed. She lay with her stern to the shore and her proud bows jutting out towards the fjord mouth. On board her, Captain Hans Mayer and Admiral Oskar Kummetz felt secure behind the screen of defences. The whole area around the fjord was alive with German land troops to guard against an attack overland. In the air, the Luftwaffe could put up fighters to ward off aerial attack while in the quiet waters of the fjord lay untold hazards for the sea-borne raider. Smoke pots on the surrounding cliffs could cover the fjord with a thick smoke-screen, making aerial attack almost out of the question.

The problem facing those who were determined to smash *Tirpitz* were great indeed but like all other difficulties there were always ways of surmounting them and it was the Royal Navy which came up with the answer. There was but one way at that time of delivering a successful attack and that was by approaching the target underwater. Any other method would be instantly discovered and inevitably end in disaster for the attackers. But a full-sized submarine would in all probability suffer a similar fate in a fjord difficult to navigate and with anti-submarine nets, not to mention the torpedo nets surrounding *Tirpitz*. A smaller type submarine capable of attacking *Tirpitz* with an explosive device other than a torpedo had to be found – and the Royal Navy had the very vessel that was required – the X-craft, the Navy's first midget submarine.

Work on a midget submarine had been going on for almost a year when, on 15 March 1942, His Majesty's Submarine X-3[1] was launched into the Hamble River, just off Southampton Water. Running low in the water under her own power she slipped into what was to be her berth, a catamaran construction with dual hulls that had been specially built as a sort of

[1] Midget submarines were all given the class X title but since there were already in existence two ships designated X, the midget submarine series had to begin with X-3.

floating dock in which X-3 could be tended and repaired out of sight of inquisitive eyes.

X-3 was a masterpiece of improvisation and invention. She was, as her name suggested, a miniature submarine. Outwardly she was similar in shape to the conventional submarine but had no conning tower. Her overall length was around fifty feet, including rudder, propeller and hydroplanes; which meant that the internal living space was restricted to only thirty-five feet, a singularly small space when one considers that it had to house a crew of three or four as well as a vast array of pipes, dials, batteries and control instruments together with its engine and all the other machinery necessary for her operation.

The diameter of the circular pressure hull at its widest point was only five and a half feet but even this was cut down because of the installation of deck boards which gave only five feet of headroom. The control room was situated for'ard and housed the steering and depth-keeping controls, the periscope together with three little scuttles each with two thicknesses of glass, two positioned on either side and one overhead. The point of these was to allow the commander to see the hull of the ship he was attacking when the periscope was not in use.

The compartment immediately aft of that comprised a chamber known as the Wet and Dry chamber. This was the escape compartment which would allow a member of the crew to leave the X-craft and re-enter using diving gear. By using this chamber a frogman, equipped with wire cutters, could leave the X-craft and cut a hole large enough in an anti-submarine net to allow the submarine through, or equipped with explosives, could attach these to the target's hull, return to the X-craft and be off before the explosive charge detonated. This innovation was also useful if the submarine got tangled up in nets or some other anti-submarine obstruction for it allowed the frogman the opportunity of freeing it.

X-3 had neither guns nor torpedoes but her 'sting' comprised explosive charges, each containing two tons of amatol, which were carried on either side of the craft. Known as 'side-cargoes' they were oblong in shape and could be detonated by a delayed action clockwork device. They were detachable and the idea was to lay them beneath the target ship.

The X-craft's diesel engine and electric motor were housed in the stern of the craft while in the bows was a compartment for stores and a tiny space for sleeping. This then was the X-craft, designed to penetrate harbours and plant its explosive load beneath the hulls of German giants ... the prototype of the X-craft which would deliver the attack on *Tirpitz* in her Norwegian lair.

While X-3 underwent trials the call was made for officers to volunteer for 'special and hazardous duty'. The men required to go to war in these tiny craft were to be of a special calibre. Service in a submarine of conventional size was often uncomfortable and difficult at the very best of times with men working in restricted space under battle conditions. Life in an X-craft was immeasurably more difficult for it demanded that men endure all the rigours of submarine attack coupled with ever-present damp and humidity as well as the inability to even stand up straight. To describe the conditions inside an X-craft as 'cramped' would be far short of the truth.

There was no shortage of volunteers, in spite of the time-worn Navy adage, 'never volunteer for anything'. None of the volunteers was given the slightest hint as to the nature of the work for which they had so eagerly volunteered. The sole stated prerequisite was that they had to be strong swimmers. Each one of them was submitted to a succession of interviews and tests, to assess both their mental and physical fitness for the job. The selection committee was given the difficult task of weeding out those who were obviously unsuitable for the job. The very slightest hint of claustrophobic tendencies was sufficient to bar a man from the course while signs of self-glorification were another reason. Above all the ideal candidates had to be stable, capable of keeping their cool in times of stress but prepared to take risks to press home an attack.

The training that followed was intense. Not a moment was wasted since speed was of the essence. No one could predict when *Tirpitz* would make a dash for the Atlantic and deny the X-craft their target. The volunteers, some of whom had never been down in a submarine, were given a crash course in the operations of the X-craft. They had to learn in a short time the intricacies of submarine navigation, of operating trim pumps, rudders and hydroplanes. They had to learn how and why the electric motors and diesel engines worked, how to recharge batteries, penetrate anti-submarine nets, negotiate minefields and master the technique of escape from a sunken submarine. All this in a desperately short time and without the slightest hint of their target or even a sight of an X-craft, for it was only after the exhaustive preliminary training that they were finally assured of a place in this select body of men. The Admiralty was leaving nothing to chance. These raw recruits, if they failed to measure up to the standards required and had to be returned from whence they came, would not do so with stories to tell. Secrecy was vital and nobody was told anything he did not absolutely have to know.

Speculation as to the purpose of all this training was rife among the volunteers. They all of them realized that the vehicle which was to take them to war was a midget submarine but what the target was or where it was remained a mystery to them. That information was reserved for those who had to know – and only them. If the slightest hint of these preparations reached the Germans the whole operation would have to be called off and years of planning and a wealth of expended energy on engineering the development of the X-craft would have been in vain.

X-3's trials quickly reached an advanced stage. She was tested and tried to the limits of her endurance and capability. Modifications were made where difficulties arose with the craft until she worked up to expectation, then a final blueprint was made for the second prototype, X-4, which was to be built at the Vickers Armstrong yard at Barrow-in-Furness under tight security. Then work began on six production types, X-5 to X-10. Again the cardinal rule was speed and work on these craft went on round the clock.

Meanwhile, operational training got under way in earnest in one of the remotest and most desolate corners of the British Isles, in Loch Striven on the west coast of Scotland. At the entrance to the loch on the Isle of Bute stood the small fishing village of Port Bannatyne which sported the Kyles Hydro Hotel, fitted out specially to house the X-craft crews.

Shortly after the arrival of the crews, X-3 and X-4, the two trials submarines, were brought to Loch Striven and the operational training got under way in earnest. With the X-craft came their mother ship the *Bonaventure*. She was specially equipped to provide a floating base for the midget submarines even to the extent of being fitted with enormous derricks, capable of lifting the X-craft right out of the water and on to her deck. Besides this she had comparatively comfortable quarters for some of the crews and offered an ideal meeting place for them after a day or night of training on the midget submarines.

There quickly grew a great sense of *esprit de corps* among the crews and evenings aboard *Bonaventure* were convivial and often boisterous.

The pace of the training hotted up. Mock attacks were made and the technique perfected but the training was not without its accidents and the first major one of these was to prove the worthiness of the crew selection.

Lieutenant John Lorimer was captain of the X-3 when the accident occurred. Acting as an instructor to two young Lieutenants, Laites and Gay, he took X-3 out one day in November 1942 on a training run. X-3 ran on the surface until she rounded the bend in Loch Striven into the exercise area and dived to begin underwater instruction. The X-craft had no sooner slipped beneath the surface than water began to pour into the control room through the induction pipe, a form of schnorkel, through which air was drawn to feed the diesel engine when cruising on diesel power at periscope depth. The valve in the pipe had failed to close securely, having jammed in the half-open position. The result was that it was open to the sea.

Within seconds, the X-craft took on an acute bow-up angle and began to slide stern-first towards the bed of the loch. Inside, Lorimer and the other two were tumbled head over heels towards the stern of the boat. Lorimer was quick to react to the situation and ordered the ballast tanks blown in a bid to get to the surface. But in the mêlée of bodies sliding around in the craft, one of the sub-lieutenants dropped the vital wheel spanner, the instrument used for blowing the tanks. The spanner slipped into the bilges and could not be recovered.

Unable to reverse her progress, the boat plunged to the loch bed and stuck fast in the mud while water continued to pour into her. Her situation was perilous indeed and had it not been for the coolness of John Lorimer, it might well have proved fatal. Their situation was made all the more dangerous because the batteries became flooded and gave off dense chlorine fumes which swiftly filled the whole boat.

X-3 lay in 100 feet of water and to make matters worse the lights went out, plunging them into darkness. Now was to be the telling time. A moment of panic in this situation would result in the accident turning into a tragedy. Lorimer remained cool with his intensive training telling him automatically what must be done. There was no hope of bringing X-3 to the surface again. That was out and he realized it. There was but one way out and that was by using their Davis Submerged Escape Apparatus. But the pressure inside the submarine would have to equal that on the outside before the hatch could be opened and it was to be an agonizingly long wait before sufficient water entered the hull to equal that pressure. In the meantime the air in the X-craft was fast becoming fouled by the chlorine fumes and it was clear that the lethal fumes would kill them all before they had a chance to escape unless they donned their DSEA without delay. Luckily there were four of these; one more than they needed, so one could be kept as a spare if one of the sets ran out.

In the pitch darkness the three men fitted on their DSEA sets then Lorimer opened the sea-cocks to speed up the intake of sea and hasten the time when the pressure inside the craft would equal that outside.

On the surface the crew of the attendant trawler *Present Help* had sensed that something was wrong and raised the alarm, bringing a variety of boats hurrying to the scene, although there was nothing they could do but wait to see what had happened and stand-by to help if the opportunity arose.

The minutes dragged slowly by for the men entombed in the X-craft. Still the water flowed in which meant that the pressure was still not equalized. It was not until the water had reached their necks that it finally stopped. Then was the time to move. Gay edged his way to the hatch and summoning all his strength, pushed it open. A deluge of water poured down on him and swept through the X-craft. In a second he was gone, streaking towards the surface, his speed regulated only by the 'apron' he held out in front of him to slow him down. Had he surfaced too quickly, he would have got a serious attack of the 'bends'.

Meanwhile, in the X-craft, Lorimer realized that all was not well with Laites. He was due to go next but he was not moving. Lorimer struggled over to him and in the darkness realized that the man was only half-conscious. His oxygen had run out. Lorimer knew that if he did not act swiftly the man would be dead. He grabbed the extra DSEA set and put it on Laites, but even the flow of pure oxygen failed to revive him. Lorimer's own oxygen supply was on the point of running out. He would have been justified in escaping himself but he was not that kind of man.

Lorimer hauled the half-conscious Laites to the hatch and

with all his remaining strength shoved him through the narrow gap. Laites shot upwards, but as he did so the DSEA set came off. By then Lorimer's oxygen had run out completely. He'd no time to waste and struggled out of the hatch. At last, with his lungs pounding in his chest, he broke surface to find willing hands grabbing him and hauling him on board *Present Help*.

All three men survived the ordeal, thanks to Lorimer's presence of mind. Had he panicked all of them would certainly have died but his training had paid off. Gay and Laites were later transferred to another branch of the Service but Lorimer opted to remain with the X-craft where he was to attain distinction in Kaa Fjord.

There were to be more accidents during these months of training and one of these brought tragedy. Lieutenant Godfrey Place, DSC, RN, was in command of X-4 one night on a training run off the stormy coast of Bute. With him were two others, Lieutenants Whitley and Thomas. The weather was atrocious and as they cruised on the surface, Thomas left the craft by the W and D (Wet and Dry) compartment to stand watch on the casing. But as he was leaving the open hatch a heavy sea pounded down on the X-craft and he was washed overboard, never to be seen again.

The sea swept into the W and D compartment and flooded it. Immediately the weight of the water in the boat made it assume a bow-up angle, pointing almost vertically towards the sky. Place could do nothing to rectify it since he had no way of blowing the flooded compartment. They just had to remain where they were until later *Present Help* arrived on the scene to rescue them.

There were other accidents during the remainder of the training time though happily none of them was fatal and while the training continued, swift progress was being made on the construction of the new X-craft, X-5 to X-10. Externally they were exactly the same as the prototypes but inside their layout was quite different. The battery compartment was for'ard. Then came the W and D compartment, the control room and at the stern the engine room. This new layout made the midget almost completely identical, in scheme at least, to the conventional submarine. But with these modifications and improvements plus the installation of additional machinery, there was even less room for the crew which made conditions even more uncomfortable for them.

Throughout all this time, there were other problems to be overcome, not the least of which was the question of how the X-craft would traverse the 1,200 miles across the sea to Kaa Fjord. The possibility of them doing so under their own steam was out of the question since first the journey would take them almost two weeks and secondly, upon their arrival the crews would be too exhausted to launch their attack. They could, too, have been taken over on board a surface ship and lowered into the water off the Norwegian coast but this would inevitably have destroyed the element of surprise, the one thing which was of paramount importance to the whole operation. It was ultimately agreed, though not until well into 1943, that each of the craft would be towed over the vast stretch of water by submarines. A 'passage crew' would man each of the X-craft while they were being towed, then at the dropping off point when the X-craft would proceed under their own power, the operational crew would take over. By this means, the men who were actually to make the attack, would undertake it fresh and alert, not having suffered the rigours of a long voyage in such a tiny craft.

The first six operational craft, X-5 to X-10, began arriving in January and February of 1943 and their base was moved from Loch Striven to one of the most desolate regions of Scotland. Loch Cairnbawn, a sea loch in the furthermost north-western tip of Scotland. There, plans were made to launch an attack on *Tirpitz* in March of that year when the Arctic darkness would provide cover for the X-craft, but this planned attack had to be abandoned almost at the last minute for a number of reasons, one of which was that 'passage crews' had not been trained up to efficiency in handling the X-craft.

The decision to postpone the operation, code-named 'Operation Source' until the autumn when conditions would once more be favourable came as a blow to the attack crews, whose whole training had been geared up to an early attack. It was clear, however, that the operation would have had disastrous consequences had it been undertaken too soon. They would, they realized, just have to wait it out until the time was right, carrying out more training exercises until all had reached a state of perfection.

In the interim period between then and the new attack date, secret agents in Norway sent intelligence reports back to

Britain, keeping the Admiralty informed of *Tirpitz*'s movements and feeding them with all the information which was so vital to the success of the operation. This was coupled with aerial photographs ferried back to Britain by reconnaissance aircraft of the Royal Air Force. Throughout these months of waiting for the crews the whole plan was taking shape. Then, at the beginning of September 1943, the first signs that the operation was imminent became apparent when all leave was cancelled and the tightest security measures were imposed at the Cairnbawn base. Suspicions that the operation was not far off were confirmed for the crews when the six towing submarines, those that would take the X-craft to the Norwegian coast, arrived in the Loch. They were *Stubborn, Sceptre, Syrtis, Sea Nymph, Thrasher* and *Truculent*. All of them had been specially fitted with the towing gear which had been designed specifically for towing the X-craft.

Immediately upon their arrival, the X-craft were allotted a towing submarine and a list of the passage and operational crews was drawn up. It read:

X-5 towed by *Thrasher* (Commanding officer A. R. Hezlet)

Passage crew:	Captain	J. H. Terry-Lloyd
	Crew	B. W. Element
		N. Garrity
Operational crew:	Captain	H. Henty-Creer
	Crew	T. J. Nelson
		D. J. Malcolm
		R. J. Mortiboys

X-6 towed by *Truculent* (Commanding officer R. L. Alexander)

Passage crew:	Captain	A. Wilson
	Crew	J. J. McGregor
		W. Oxley
Operational crew:	Captain	D. Cameron
	Crew	J. T. Lorimer
		R. H. Kendall
		E. Goddard

X-7 towed by *Stubborn* (Commanding officer A. A. Duff)

Passage crew:	Captain	P. H. Philip
	Crew	J. Magennis
		F. Luck

Operational crew:	Captain	B. C. G. Place
	Crew	L. B. C. Whittam
		R. Aitken
		W. M. Whitley

X-8 towed by *Sea Nymph* (Commanding officer J. P. H. Oakley)

Passage crew:	Captain	J. Smart
	Crew	W. H. Pomeroy
		J. G. Robinson
Operational crew:	Captain	B. M. McFarlane
	Crew	W. Y. Marsden
		R. X. Hindmarsh
		J. B. Murray

X-9 towed by *Syrtis* (Commanding officer M. B. Jupp)

Passage crew:	Captain	E. A. Kearon
	Crew	A. H. Harte
		G. H. Hollis
Operational crew:	Captain	T. L. Martin
	Crew	J. Brooks
		V. Coles
		M. Shean

X-10 towed by *Sceptre* (Commanding officer I. S. McIntosh)

Passage crew:	Captain	E. V. Page
	Crew	J. Fishleigh
		A. Brookes
Operational crew:	Captain	K. R. Hudspeth
	Crew	B. Enzer
		G. G. Harding
		L. Tilley

The passage crews comprised only three members since a diver was not required.

Preparations were going by them at a furious pace and the day soon arrived when the six X-craft were hoisted aboard *Bonaventure* to have their side-charges fitted, an operation which almost brought 'Source', the six X-craft and *Bonaventure* to an untimely and tragic end. While one of the two-ton amatol charges was being fitted to X-6, a workman was busily using a welding torch nearby. A spark from it started a fire among the

other charges lying on deck. The very sight of a fire among all
that explosive was enough to send the workmen dashing away
from it but fortunately John Lorimer, who was supervising
the operation, showed his remarkable coolness once more by
grabbing a hose and with the aid of another officer extinguish-
ing the flames. Had the explosives ignited, the result would certainly have been the instant disappearance of *Bonaventure* and
all and everything on board her. It was later discovered however that the amatol, far from exploding, would merely have
melted since it required a detonator to explode it. This knowledge, however, did little to calm the taut nerves of the workmen.

Fortunately there were no more nasty incidents in these last
few days before Saturday, 11 September 1943, when at 4 p.m.
His Majesty's Submarine X-3 under tow by the submarine
Truculent left Loch Cairnbawn, followed closely by the other
five X-craft. 'Operation Source' was under way. With years of
planning and tiring months of training behind them, the crews
of the X-craft were finally on their way to war.

But even then, after Admiral Barry, the mastermind behind
the planning of Source, had given the order to go, there was still
some doubt as to whether *Tirpitz* could be hit ... and even as
to where she was! At the time of their leaving Cairnbawn,
Tirpitz was at sea with her attendant vessels and there was no
guarantee that she would return to Kaa Fjord, so alternative
plans of attack had to be formulated in the event that she might
drop anchor elsewhere. Only at the last moment would the X-
craft crews know for sure where they were to launch their
attack.

The agonies suffered by the men who formed the passage
crews of the X-craft were terrible. The six towing submarines
travelled in roughly six parallel courses pulling their 'ugly
ducklings' behind them and keeping these small boats in a
balanced trim was verging on the impossible. They tended to
'porpoise', passing through the water in a wave-like form of
movement, performing something like underwater acrobatics
and inducing in the crews the worst possible kind of sea-sick-
ness. Besides the awful conditions under which they made the
journey they had also to keep the boat in perfect working order
for the operational crew which was to take over. Instruments
and the machinery had to be checked constantly to ensure that
they were still in working order. These men played a crucial

part in the whole operation since, if the X-craft were not in perfect working order when they were handed over, they would be useless for the attack. All this, coupled with complete lack of proper sleep, was very wearing on the nerves.

For four days the small fleet of boats coursed on towards Norway, with the X-craft surfacing only occasionally to take in fresh air and refresh the tired and exhausted crews. Then on the fifth day a signal from the Admiralty clinched their objective. It revealed that *Tirpitz* had in fact returned to Kaa Fjord but with her she had brought other worthy targets in the shape of the battle-cruiser *Scharnhorst* and the pocket battleship *Lützow*. *Scharnhorst* lay at anchor just inside the anti-submarine nets which straddled the entry to Kaa Fjord, while *Lützow* lay anchored in Langefjord, a narrow stretch of water which, like Kaa Fjord, was an extension of Altenfjord. This knowledge brought into operation Target Plan Four in which X-5, X-6 and X-7 would attack *Tirpitz*, while X-9 and X-10 attacked *Scharnhorst*, and X-8 *Lützow*.

That then was the basic plan of operation but it was in for some radical changes before it took place. Disaster was to strike Operation Source. The tow rope linking X-9 with *Syrtis* broke and the X-craft was lost with all hands. If that were not enough, more was to follow when X-8 was forced to jettison both her side charges each of which blew up when they reached the ocean bed and on each occasion they caused X-8 damage and she had to be scuttled. Her crew was taken on board the parent submarine *Sea Nymph*. Both *Syrtis* and *Sea Nymph* changed course north to safe positions where they could radio the Admiralty and report their losses and await further instructions.

On the 19th, the operational crews took over from the weary and exhausted men who had brought the craft over the thousand miles. By then they were well inside the Arctic Circle and making good progress but their troubles were only beginning. The most formidable part of their voyage was nearing as they approached their 'slipping off' point, the position where they would part from their respective parent submarines. The 20th was the day chosen for the craft to part company and it was one which began and continued with troubles which almost brought the operation to an end.

Early that morning *Stubborn* was nosing towards the point at which she would part with X-7 when a lookout on the bridge spotted a mine floating off her starboard bow. It was close and coming closer, floating freely on the surface and riding down the entire length of the submarine only feet away from the hull. At any second one of its horns might touch the casing, just enough to blow her up; but it continued on its way, nudged the tow line between the submarine and the X-craft, ran down its length and came to rest jammed at the point where the tow line joined the X-craft's bows. Men both on the submarine and the X-craft watched transfixed, some hardly able to move. The slightest touch and there would be an almighty explosion which would send not only X-7, but *Stubborn* as well, to the bottom. Godfrey Place, with a coolness which is still the talk of the ward room, made his way along the casing and found that the mine's mooring wire had got entangled in the tow rope. With all eyes fixed on his every move, he calmly went about the business of untangling it. It took him all of seven minutes to free the mine before he nonchalantly placed a foot on it and shoved it away from his craft, followed by loud cheering from the relieved onlookers.

From this point on and to get a clear picture of the events that followed it is best to follow the fortunes of each of the craft individually right up to the point of attack. One of them, X-10, was destined not to make an attack at all. She reached a point three miles from her target, the *Scharnhorst*, but because of severe mechanical trouble, her commander, Lieutenant Hudspeth, was forced to give up the attempt and return to the open sea where he joined up again with his parent submarine.

X-5, under the command of Lieutenant Henty-Creer, seems to have succeeded in penetrating all but the final defences. She reached Kaa Fjord, only to be sighted by *Tirpitz* and sunk by gunfire and depth charges. None of her crew survived.

The whole operation so far had been dogged with misfortune and there remained only two X-craft to press home the attack, X-6, under Donald Cameron, and X-7, commanded by Godfrey Place.

In the early evening of 20 September, X-6 was slipped from her tow and proceeded under her own power into the Söröy Sound, leaving her parent submarine to retreat out to sea and lie in wait for her return from the mission. Cameron successfully negotiated the Söröy minefield and nosed X-6 into Altenfjord to begin the forty-mile voyage towards Kaa Fjord and *Tirpitz*. Besides the myriad obstacles that lay in their path,

Cameron encountered difficulty in keeping X-6 in trim. This difficulty was caused by flows of fresh water which the boat crept into, and since this did not afford the same degree of buoyancy she quickly lost her trim.

The night that followed was not without incident. X-6 steered for the group of small Brattholm islands but not before her periscope became flooded and Cameron found himself nosing his way up the fjord almost blind. Lying amid the small group of islands while she recharged her batteries, she was forced to dive several times during the night when German ships appeared and on one occasion she was almost rammed by one of them when a steering defect prevented Lorimer, the officer of the watch, from getting far enough out of the way.

At 1.45 a.m. on Wednesday, 22 September, X-6 slipped out of her island haven towards the mouth of Kaa Fjord with Cameron navigating by dead reckoning. As the craft slipped nearer to the anti-submarine nets – the first major obstacle to getting into Kaa Fjord – Kendall, the boat's diver, began donning his frogman's suit. It would be his job, when the nets were reached, to leave the craft via the W and D compartment and, by the use of electrically powered cutters, fashion a hole in the net through which X-6 could sail.

The tension in the craft mounted as she drew closer to the nets. By 4 a.m. they were within half a mile of them and the sun was rising over the towering mountains which formed the giant walls of the fjord. Cameron brought X-6 to periscope depth and peered through the eye-piece, only to find that his periscope had flooded once more. Now he would, it seemed, have to ride it to the target blind. This posed many difficulties, not the least of which was the possibility of detection.

Cameron ordered X-6 down to sixty feet and set course to collide with the nets, but as she eased forward Cameron caught the sound of propeller blades thrashing in the water above him. Quickly he brought X-6 back to periscope depth and in a fleeting glimpse through the periscope before she became flooded again, he caught sight of a trawler heading for the net. This could mean but one thing – that the 'gate' in the net, which allowed surface ships through, was open. It was an opportunity not to be missed. Cameron realized that if he remained submerged and travelling on battery power his speed would be insufficient to keep up with the trawler and he would reach the nets as the gate was being closed. There was but one way to slip through the gate and that was on the surface. It was a bold and daring move.

'Surface!' Cameron ordered. 'Full ahead diesel.'

The deck of X-6 broke surface and she trailed behind the trawler through the net gate and once through Cameron quickly ordered her to dive. He had, it seemed, pulled it off and remained unseen. They were inside the battleship's lair but Cameron cursed his luck for the periscope had flooded again and they were blind once more.

He was so close to his target that he dared not let anything hinder him in his attack so he took X-6 down to seventy feet and got to work on the faulty periscope. But try as he might he could do nothing to rectify the fault, since the leak was on the outside. However, he cleaned it out and took another look through it, only to find himself amid a concentration of enemy warships of all shapes and sizes. He was right inside the hornets' nest and caught a glimpse of *Tirpitz*, sitting majestically at anchor with her superstructure towering high into the sky.

From then on, Cameron had to approach *Tirpitz* by dead reckoning to overcome the final obstacle, the anti-torpedo nets which surrounded her. Slipping through the water at a mere two knots, it took almost an hour to get close to the nets. Then Cameron decided to risk another glance through the faulty periscope.

X-6 rose to periscope depth and Cameron peered through the eye-piece. His reaction to what he saw was instant. Only feet away from where they were was the towering hull of a German destroyer and X-6 was nosing towards her on a collision course. Cameron ordered Lorimer, operating the controls, to dive; and the response was immediate. X-6 sped into the depths, narrowly missing the enemy warship.

Cameron shut off the motors and kept a silent watch for the sound of enemy ships attacking them. It seemed certain that they had been spotted but after a lengthy pause, no sound reached them. They had not been seen. Again Cameron brought X-6 to periscope depth but as the periscope was retracted after he had a glimpse through it, the electric motor powering the periscope short-circuited and caught fire. Cameron took her down to sixty feet and fought the fire with an extinguisher, dousing the flames but leaving the craft filled with choking smoke.

It seemed that they were doomed to failure but they had got

that far and none of the crew was about to give up at that stage. They resolved to press on with the attack even with the hindrance of a partially flooded periscope which had now to be raised by hand and a steadily increasing list caused by water seeping into one of the side charges. The craft was seriously crippled and in fact in no condition to carry out the attack; but dogged determination drove all on board on.

Cameron, using the X-craft's glass ports to guide him through the water, brought his boat towards the northern shore of the fjord; but as he did so there was a sudden jolt and a loud scraping sound. She had hit something which, through the glass ports, looked like a pontoon of some description. Cameron took his boat away from the obstacle and dived deep in a bid to travel underneath the torpedo nets around *Tirpitz* but instead of doing so he rammed straight into them. He backed off and brought X-6 to periscope depth and had a quick look at his surroundings. As he swung the clouded periscope around he caught sight of a German picket boat entering the 'gate' in the nets. This was the answer to his prayers. He'd managed to squirm through the anti-submarine nets at the mouth of the fjord and now he was determined to pull off a 'double'.

At five minutes past seven that morning X-6 slipped through the gate behind the unsuspecting picket boat and dived out of sight. But as the boat shot downwards it careered into a sunken rock and everyone inside was bowled over. Cameron ordered full astern and the boat charged backwards and for a moment broke the surface of the water. This time however their luck was out and she was spotted by a sailor on the deck of *Tirpitz* who reported the sighting to an officer. Amazingly the officer discounted the sighting as a large fish or perhaps a log which had broken surface. Cameron's luck was in!

Back beneath the surface once more, Cameron prepared for the run-in on *Tirpitz*. He aimed X-6 to hit the battleship astern and run along her length dropping his side charges as he went. The run should have taken two minutes but when after a three-minute interval he had failed to hit *Tirpitz*, he ordered X-6 to periscope depth. When she rose she actually broke surface once more and this time there was no mistaking her for a fish or a floating log. The alarm went off in *Tirpitz*.

Moments after this, as X-6 dived, she became entangled in a thick wire dangling over the side of *Tirpitz* while seamen on board the battleship opened fire with an assortment of small arms and threw hand grenades overboard. X-6 managed to struggle free of the wire and immediately shot to the surface once more to come under intensive attack from the grenades and small arms fire which pinged off her casing.

Cameron and the others in the craft realized only too well that they hadn't a hope of escaping from the fjord. The stretch of water was crammed with destroyers and anti-submarine ships which would blast her out of the water with depth charges. The element of surprise had been lost. All thoughts of escape had to be banished from their minds. Only the attack mattered now. X-6 dodged under the keel of *Tirpitz* and Cameron dropped his four tons of explosives, set to go off in an hour's time. He was not to know it then, but his were not the only explosives ticking away under the *Tirpitz*'s keel.

Only minutes after the charges had been dropped, X-6 broke surface and her crew spilled on to the deck having burned their secret documents. The machine-gun and rifle fire which had sprayed the craft ceased. A launch drew alongside and the four submariners clambered aboard it while a tow rope was secured to the X-craft. But as the launch moved off, the German crew became aware that the X-craft was sinking away from them. Before leaving the craft Cameron had opened her sea-cocks and set the controls to dive, with the engine still running. One of the German seamen slashed the rope and the X-craft disappeared beneath the surface.

Cameron and the others were thereupon taken on board *Tirpitz*, the battleship underneath which lay eight tons of amatol explosive set to explode in less than an hour. Four tons of this powerful explosive had already been set by Godfrey Place in X-7.

Lieutenant Place's sojourn into Altenfjord and subsequently into Kaa Fjord had been no less eventful than Cameron's. He had brought X-7 up the forty-mile long Altenfjord in much the same way as X-6 had made the voyage but on his journey he was constantly bothered by shipping traffic and at one point narrowly missed being rammed. He successfully negotiated the anti-submarine nets but his luck ran out when he reached the anti-torpedo nets around *Tirpitz*. X-7 became hopelessly entangled in these nets and seemingly caught fast and unable to shake herself free.

Place tried every move in the book to wriggle free, including flooding the inboard tanks in a bid to drop out of the nets, but his effort was in vain. For a solid hour he struggled to get out of the entanglement until without warning X-7 broke loose and shot to the surface. Surely, Place thought, they must have been seen; but there was no sound of pursuing destroyers or depth charges when they dived again for another attempt at getting through the nets. He went deep and tried to slip beneath the nets but again he got caught and had to fight his way free. Once more he tried, this time at an even greater depth; but again he got caught and managed to struggle free. It seemed that he was fated to go no farther and he decided to bring X-7 to periscope depth and look around and sum up the situation. When he did so, however, he discovered to his amazement that he was on the *inside* of the nets and in an ideal position for an attack. How his craft had got through the nets was, and still is, a mystery but he was indeed there and that was precisely where he wanted to be.

Place estimated that he was almost thirty feet from *Tirpitz* and he set course for his attack. Seconds later the little craft slammed into the giant's side, about twenty feet beneath the surface, and slid along her, dropping the side charges; then Place headed to the position where he had succeeded in penetrating the anti-torpedo nets. But try as he might he could not get through. By then Cameron in X-6 had been captured and the Germans, realizing that he might not be alone, were busily dropping depth charges in a bid to thwart any other attempts on the ship.

Place was penned in behind the nets and it was simply a matter of time before he was blasted to kingdom come by the depth charges. He decided to bring X-7 to periscope depth to discover if there was another way out. All around the craft while she rose to the surface, the water was a torment as the charges exploded, and when Place reached the surface he found the X-7 was *half-way across the top of the nets*. X-7 slipped over, spotted by the Germans who opened fire on her, then she disappeared underwater between the inner and the middle nets where again she became entangled. Place fought to free the craft; ever aware that his explosive charges would be going off at any moment yet there was little he could do about it. X-7 was firmly caught in the nets. The minutes passed and the struggle continued but then the time ran out. An almighty explosion threw the X-craft clear of the nets. The amatol had exploded under *Tirpitz*. By some miracle X-7 sustained no serious damage in the explosion but the depth charges were exploding dangerously close. Again it was only a matter of time before he would be found. Place appreciated that he was imprisoned in the fjord. There was no alternative but to abandon ship and reluctantly he decided to surrender. This at least would save the lives of his crew.

Place brought X-7 to the surface and opened the hatch in the control room, then waved a white sweater out of it in a sign of surrender. Guns from many of the boats in the vicinity had been trained on the tiny portion of the craft which showed above the water but the firing stopped when the white 'flag' of surrender showed itself. Place clambered on to the deck, continuing to wave his flag of surrender but he had no sooner stood upright than the craft hit a battle practice target and sea poured in through the open hatch before Place had a chance of slamming it closed. The weight of the inflowing water sent the X-craft careering to the bottom of the fjord while Place clung on to the practice target, unable to do anything to help his crew. Sadly only Sub-Lieutenant Aitken succeeded in escaping from the stricken X-craft as it lay on the bottom, and both he and Place were taken prisoner.

The cost of the operation in terms of lives lost was high but *Tirpitz* had sustained serious damage; so serious in fact that she was unable to move from her anchorage for a further seven months during which time she was again damaged by a Fleet Air Arm Attack. She had been severely crippled and was taken south to Tromsö for further repairs. While she was there, the Royal Air Force delivered the *coup de grâce* when the famous Dam Buster Squadron bombed her. A near miss caused her to roll over at her anchorage and she lay wedged in the mud with only her keel sticking above the water's surface. *Tirpitz* was finished for ever.

The survivors of Operation Source spent the remainder of the war in captivity, unaware of how successful their attack had been. It was only after they were flown back to Britain that they learned of their success. Those two tiny craft and their crews had crippled Germany's biggest warship to such an extent that she had no longer a remote hope of putting to sea again as a fighting ship.

For their part in pressing home that daring raid Lieutenant Donald Cameron, RNVR and Lieutenant (now Rear-Admiral)

Godfrey Place, RN were awarded the Victoria Cross. Their citation ended:

'The courage, endurance and utter contempt for danger in the immediate face of the enemy shown by Lieutenants Place and Cameron during this determined and successful attack were supreme.'

The extent of the success of Operation Source was not immediately apparent because, although *Tirpitz* had been badly holed, she remained on an even keel and the Germans went to great lengths to ensure that aerial reconnaissance photographs of her would not reveal that she had been seriously crippled. It was not until Norwegian Resistance reports filtered through to the Admiralty that it became clear *Tirpitz* had been dealt a critical wound. It was only when confirmation of the success of the attack was received that the Admiralty's faith in its X-craft was justified and serious plans could be made for further operations.

More X-craft were built incorporating modifications to improve their handling during attack and refinements were made coupled with changes in attack procedures, the basic one being that in future operations would be launched on a 'one target, one X-craft' basis. There would in future be no multiple attacks on a single enemy vessel.

There remained, however, in spite of the success of the *Tirpitz* raid, a niggling doubt in the minds of those who had been rather sceptical about the potential of the X-craft. The essence of an X-craft attack was to carry it out and return to its parent submarine safely. None of them so far had succeeded in doing that, but the day was not far off when such a raid would be carried out and on a target more easily defended than the *Tirpitz* herself. The target was the Laksevaag floating dock which lay in the Norwegian harbour of Bergen, and the craft chosen to undertake the attack was one of the new modified midget submarines, the X-24 under the command of Lieutenant Max Shean, RANVR.

To reach its target, X-24 had to penetrate the heavily-defended Hjeltefjord, West Byfjord and Puddefjord before reaching Bergen which lay tucked away in the latter of the three fjords. Apart from being protected by myriad defences, these fjords were continually patrolled by boats fitted with sonar devices for the detection of submarine craft and it was also the busiest stretch of water in Norway.

X-24 left the Shetlands with its operational crew on board on 11 April 1944, having left her base some days earlier operated by a passage crew. The passage from the Shetlands across the North Sea passed without event and at the appointed time two and a half days later she slipped off from her parent submarine *Sceptre* and nosed into the first of the fjords, negotiating a minefield as she went. Their passage from there to the target area was beset with hazards, not the least of which were the anti-submarine patrol boats which on two occasions picked X-24 up on their Asdic. It was only by some deft zig-zag manoeuvring that Shean avoided being blown to bits by depth charges. His skill as a commander during that passage was tested to the limit for he had to elude barrages of searchlights which swept the water at strategic points. Perhaps his greatest hazard was the very volume of traffic in the fjords. It seemed that every conceivable kind of craft was plying these waters, which made operating at periscope depth a particularly dangerous business. On more than one occasion, Shean just narrowly avoided being rammed.

When he arrived at the floating dock, Shean found a merchant ship lying alongside her. Determined to make absolutely sure of hitting his target he coolly carried out two practice runs on it before dropping his side charges and retreating. The attack went perfectly, or so it seemed, and X-24 rendezvoused with *Sceptre* at the appointed place and returned to Britain. The reception given to the crew of X-24 matched the best traditions of the navy. But alas, the rejoicing over Shean's success was premature. Intelligence reports which were received indicated that the dock still remained intact, although the merchant ship had been blown to bits. Shean was desperately disappointed. Pure coincidence had foiled his attempt at a successful attack.

Before he had left, he had been given strict instructions to use his periscope as few times as possible while in the target area. Shean had stuck to these instructions and attacked the target 'blind', sighting the underwater part of the 'dock' by means of the glass scuttle. The tragedy of the operation was that the hull of the merchantman was exactly the same length as that of the dock and Shean had mistaken it for the dock and dropped his charges under the wrong one. Although very disappointed at not hitting the correct target, Shean had consolation in the knowledge that he had penetrated an enemy harbour, laid charges and returned unscathed; and in doing so proved that it could be done. But that was not the end of the story. The Navy was still determined to wreck the floating dock and on 11 September that year, X-24 returned to Bergen, this time under the command of Lieutenant Westmacott, RN. There was no mistake on this occasion and the floating dock, as well as another merchant ship, was sunk.

Later that year, X-craft took part in the preparations for the D-day landings when they carried out underwater reconnaissance sorties along the northern coast of France, feeding back vital information about the beaches, depths of water etc. where the landings were to take place. But it was in a far different clime that the X-craft, or more correctly the XE-craft, were to take their final bow with devastating effect.

Specially adapted craft, designated XE-craft, were built for operations in the Far East. Since they were required to operate in a very hot climate, they incorporated special refrigeration units and air-conditioning systems as well as an engine-cooling system. At the beginning of 1945, six of these craft were transported to Australia on the redoubtable mother ship *Bonaventure*.

The most spectacular operation following their arrival in the Far East took place at the end of July. The Japanese heavy cruisers *Takao* and *Myoko* lay in the Straits of Jahore, the narrow strip of water between the island of Singapore and the mainland of Malaya. The plan was that two XE-craft were to be towed to a pre-arranged point then slipped off. From there they would carry on independently, XE-1 (Lieutenant J. E. Smart) to attack the *Myoko* and XE-3 (Lieutenant Ian Fraser) to attack the *Takao*.

Both commanders studied the plan carefully and examined the available charts so that they knew exactly how they would go about their respective attacks and also familiarize themselves with the attack plans of the other commander.

Fraser's mission was perhaps the trickier of the two because the *Takao* was lying in very shallow water with depths ranging from only eleven to seventeen feet. She did, however, lie over a depression in the sea-bed with her bow and stern in water which at low tide dropped to less than three feet.

Fraser decided that he would have to pass over the shallows

and dive into the depression to place his explosives. With the depression only 500 feet across and 1,500 feet long, it did not afford him much room to manoeuvre his boat. He was firmly convinced that the task that had been set him was impossible but this deterred neither him nor his crew from willingly undertaking it. His tiny craft left *Bonaventure* under tow by the parent submarine *Stygian* while XE-1 and her parent submarine also put to sea.

At 11 p.m. on 30 July, the XE-craft changed hands and the operational crew took over from the passage crew; then the two XE-craft slipped their tows and set course for their respective targets.

The commanders and crews of both XE-craft were to distinguish themselves that night but it is with the exploits of XE-3 under the command of Ian Fraser that we are concerned here, because for the men of that craft the attack was to be fraught with the most unbelievable danger.

Fraser stood on the boat's casing as he guided her on the surface through the first of the obstacles he was to encounter that night – a minefield. Seemingly unperturbed, he navigated the craft through the mines that bobbed on the surface, held fast by their long anchor chains. One touch on the slender horns which jutted out of these mines and the mission would be brought abruptly to a halt.

Black clouds hid the moon and made navigation difficult, but Fraser continued to feel his way forward through the darkness until he approached a point where he knew the Japs had positioned listening posts. He stopped engines and slid forward under battery power, every inch of the way waiting for the telltale boom of gunfire that would signal exposure or the slender finger of a searchlight that would bathe him in light. But luckily neither came and, once through the danger zone, Fraser started engines again and pressed on once more, altering position as best he could to keep him on the right course for his target.

XE-3 had not gone far when Fraser, still on the outer casing, caught sight of an object not far ahead of him which he took to be a buoy. He steered towards it and to his horror discovered that it was no buoy but a fishing boat. He barked an order to the helmsman, E. R. A. Reed, and XE-3 swept away from the boat, apparently unnoticed by the fishermen on board.

The crew heaved a sigh of relief when the danger was past

but an hour later they were to encounter more trouble. Fraser's eyes pierced the inky darkness and spotted two more ships approaching at speed, and he dived quickly to avoid being spotted, remaining on the bottom until the throb of engines had passed.

On they went with Fraser gingerly slipping deeper into the Jahore Straits until the craft nosed through the defence boom which it appeared was kept permanently open. Then at 12.50 a.m. Fraser sighted *Takao* sitting motionless in the still water. The flat calm of the water was to make the attack all the more difficult. If he were to make his run-in with periscope up, the trail left by the periscope would undoubtedly betray his presence to a lookout and probably spell disaster for himself and his crew. He had no alternative but to rely on quick periscope checks to get his bearings and make course corrections.

Ahead of XE-3 sat the Japanese cruiser, and the pre-attack tension mounted as Fraser closed in on her. He brought her to periscope depth and took a final glimpse through it before running in for the attack; but through the eye-piece Fraser saw a Japanese launch crammed with troops only yards away and sailing between him and his target.

Perspiration poured off his brow. XE-3 was already late for the attack and the tide was on the wane. There was no time to waste since he was fast running out of depth in which to carry out the attack. But there was no turning back now and minutes later XE-3 hit the *Takao* about the level of the bilge keel and towards the stern of the cruiser. Instantly the craft bounced down the cruiser's side and stuck firmly in the mud.

Fraser was not satisfied that he was in the best position to place his explosive charges and plant his limpet mines, so he struggled out of the mud, throwing great clouds of it up to the surface as he did so and creating a fearful din. By some fluke, the noise was not heard on board the cruiser, otherwise an immediate counter-attack would have followed.

Once free of the mud, XE-3 backed off again and Fraser brought her to periscope depth for a glimpse at the target. Then he lined up on *Takao*'s forward funnel. Straining his eyes, he could see the *Takao*'s hull looming up in front of him. Then in a few seconds there was blackness as the XE-craft slipped beneath the cruiser and into the depression beneath her. XE-3 was perfectly positioned to drop her charges but the tide was falling quickly and the space between *Takao*'s keel and the deck of XE-3 was decreasing fast.

The cruiser was a mere foot above the midget's casing and Fraser allowed his crew to peer through the periscope at their target. But they had no time to linger. There was work to be done and it had to be done quickly before they got trapped in the depression.

Fraser set about releasing his main charge, two tons of explosives contained in a side cargo; but he soon found that it was stuck fast and would not budge. It seemed that that form of attack was out of the question. His alternative was to attach limpet mines to the cruiser's hull and Leading Seaman Magennis, the XE-craft's diver, was already pulling on his rubber suit and donning his breathing apparatus.

Magennis made his way into the W and D compartment, closed the connecting hatch and flooded the compartment but when he tried to open the escape hatch he found that he could open it only half-way – the lid was hard up against the *Takao*'s keel. Undaunted, he removed his breathing apparatus and barely managed to squeeze out of the hatch trailing his oxygen bottles behind him. Once outside he struggled into the apparatus again – a feat that had never before been performed by a diver in action.

Magennis set about the business of attaching the six limpet mines which he had retrieved from their housing on XE-3's side, to the hull of the Jap cruiser. But the hull was a mass of razor sharp shells, barnacles and seaweed and he found that the limpets would not stick to it. The magnets used for attaching would not hold on the surface so he set about chipping away the barnacles with his knife, slashing his hands in the process. Only after an agonizing struggle did he succeed in clearing a space to attach the mines but it had taken him all of half an hour to do so and with the mines firmly locked on to the cruiser, he returned to the XE-craft and barely managed to struggle in through the hatch once more, again repeating the operation of removing his breathing apparatus before entering.

Now that Magennis was back in the craft Fraser tried again to release the port side cargo and this time it slid off to settle on the bottom, ideally positioned to effect the maximum damage to *Takao*. But when he tried to repeat the operation with the starboard side cargo, he found it solidly jammed. Try as he and the others might he could not budge it. With the seconds ticking away and the chances of detection heightening as they passed, Fraser decided that it was time to go with or without the limpet-carrier.

He ordered full astern and the engines groaned to pull the craft away but nothing happened. XE-3 was stuck fast. Fraser tried moving the helm first in one direction and then in the other in a bid to wriggle free but it was all to no avail. In a final desperate bid to get free of the *Takao* before he and the crew were crushed to death Fraser blew the main ballast tanks and the XE-craft shot backwards and rocketed to the surface, breaking water only a few yards from yet another Jap launch carrying troops. Immediately Fraser dived again, apparently unseen by the Japs but still after all their cavorting about underwater the limpet-carrier would not free itself and the boat soon got out of control, doing nothing but running in circles because of the heavy weight on the starboard side.

There was no alternative but for one of the crew to don a frogman's suit and go out to prise the limpet-carrier free. Fraser decided he would go but Magennis was not having it. He was the diver, he intimated, and he would go. So once more, still exhausted and suffering from badly cut hands, Magennis entered the W and D compartment, this time armed with a huge spanner. Soon he was outside and thumping and hauling away at the offending piece of machinery. After fifteen minutes of gruelling work, the carrier at last slipped free and Magennis was able to return to the midget submarine. He was in such a state of utter exhaustion that he had to be pulled bodily from the W and D compartment.

With his job done, Fraser made all speed to get clear of the area and as far down the Jahore Straits as he could before the balloon went up. As he did so there was an almighty explosion and the bottom was ripped out of the *Takao*. Fraser's mission was completed and XE-3 met up with *Stygian* and was towed back to *Bonaventure* and a hero's welcome.

Lieutenant Smart in XE-1 had not been so lucky in his attack. He was delayed many times by enemy patrol boat activity and forced to abandon his mission so he was determined not to return with his side cargoes. Without knowing whether or not Fraser had laid his explosives, Smart took his craft alongside *Takao* and dropped his, then set course out of the target area.

For their courage during the attack on *Takao*, both Fraser and Magennis were awarded the Victoria Cross. This was the last major X-craft operation carried out by the Royal Navy before the end of the Second World War but there was one other which merits mention because it proved the versatility of the X-craft as a weapon. It occurred at the same time as the attack on the Japanese cruisers when XE-craft severed the underwater communication cables linking Singapore, Saigon and Hong Kong. Two XE-craft took part in the operation commanded by the same men who had attacked the floating dock at Bergen: Shean and Westmacott.

The XE-craft had in fact arrived too late in the Far East to play any decisive part in the defeat of the Japanese Navy, much to the dismay of the men who served in them.

Conclusion

The dropping of two atomic bombs brought about the end to the Second World War and with the advent of the bomb there came a whole new concept in warfare. With atomic bombs in sufficient numbers, a power could start a war and win it in only a few days. Indeed the possession of the bomb was, *in the right hands,* a deterrent to global warfare and a powerfully persuasive political weapon. The United States had that deterrent and demonstrated that she would use it if the need arose.

It was the Soviet Union, once an ally, which became the potential aggressor and threatened world peace. But the Russians knew they could never hope to win a conflict with the West or greatly influence the political future of the world without an atomic armoury. Then in 1953, they exploded an atomic bomb and the possibility of a third world war of cataclysmic dimensions become frighteningly close to reality.

The race for nuclear superiority was on. More powerful atomic and subsequently hydrogen bombs were manufactured. Rockets and aircraft were designed to deliver them. Sophisticated early warning systems were devised and anti-missile missiles placed at strategic points to counter a nuclear attack.

The ability to deliver the nuclear package successfully through the defence systems and on to target was of cardinal importance. In the United States, giant bombers of Strategic Air Command armed with nuclear weapons kept a constant state of readiness. On the ground long-range rockets, some visible and others housed in silos, could be fired across the span of an ocean on to targets in Russia – and of course the reverse was true. However, neither of these systems was infallible; both the rockets and the aircraft could be detected by the early warning systems and, if traced in time, possibly destroyed before they reached their targets. It was clear then that the element of surprise, so absolutely crucial to achieving the first strike advantage in a nuclear attack, could be lost, giving the enemy an opportunity of retaliating both with his offensive and defensive weapons. In the event of both sides' nuclear devices reaching their targets the result would almost certainly have been the total contamination of the globe.

In terms of rocket attack, the United Kingdom is on Russia's doorstep and therefore so much more vulnerable to fast, surprise attack. If Russia were to have waged war on the West then Britain would have been a prime target. To counter the Soviet menace and also ensure a second strike capability as well as surprise superiority some other form of delivery to target had to be found. The United States Navy sought the answer in the submarine, armed with nuclear rockets. No other form of launch system could match the submarine for mobility and invisibility. The strategists envisaged an almost complete change of role for the submarine. No longer would its primary task be that of attacking ships at sea; now its role was to be that of mobile rocket launcher, hitting a target within enemy territory. In addition, it would have to remain submerged on patrol for long periods of time to make it elusive and less easily detected. If that were achieved then the enemy could not be certain from which point he was likely to be attacked. Nuclear power was to make all this possible in a most dramatic way.

The answer to the problem of very long submerged patrols came first when the United States built and completed the nuclear powered submarine *Nautilus* in 1954. She achieved a success far beyond the wildest dreams of the most ardent protagonists of the system. She was conventionally armed with twenty torpedoes and her performance was little short of a marvel. Her power was derived from a nuclear reactor which produced heat from which steam was generated to drive her turbines. She could operate independently of her home base and patrol almost indefinitely under nuclear power.

Among her most staggering achievements was *Nautilus'* voyage from Hawaii under the Polar ice cap to Britain in 1958. This is the shortest route and the entire voyage was undertaken completely submerged. (Since then, the American nuclear-powered submarine *Triton* has circumnavigated the world without surfacing. Patrols lasting two or more months are now a matter of course.) Because the nuclear submarine does not require fresh air to enable its engines to function, it does not need to surface regularly. An air purification system enables the crew to live comfortably for prolonged periods while submerged. And since the nuclear submarine has no need to surface, the chances of her detection by enemy radar are slim indeed, although she can still be traced by Sonar and Asdic devices. However, her high speed, which can be far in excess of twenty knots, makes evasion from attack so much easier. It also enables the torpedo-equipped nuclear submarine to make an attack and be well out of the danger area before retaliatory action is taken. The problem of long-duration submerged patrols had been overcome.

The United States continued to build nuclear submarines and indeed stopped production of their more conventionally propelled boats. In the United Kingdom, the Royal Navy kept a keen watch upon the progress of American nuclear submarine developments and when Admiral Mountbatten was appointed First Sea Lord in 1955, the building of Britain's first nuclear submarine, *Dreadnought*, was authorized. Like the US Navy's first nuclear submarine, *Dreadnought* was armed with torpedoes and was developed as a counter measure to the nuclear submarine. She was launched in 1960 and commissioned in 1963. However, steps were afoot in the United States which were radically to alter the status of the submarine.

The project which was destined to revolutionize the role of the submarine was known as the Polaris system. This was the second string to the nuclear bow and envisaged a nuclear-powered submarine equipped with sixteen intercontinental ballistic missiles, each one capable of striking targets up to 2,500 miles inside the Soviet Union. The first of these missiles was fired in a test launch from the USS *George Washington* while she was submerged in July 1960. The combination of nuclear-powered submarine and nuclear rocket strike capability had been realized.

It was not until 1963 that the Royal Navy finally adopted the Polaris system and in doing so became a major submarine power. Today she has four Polaris submarines which patrol the oceans ready at a moment's notice to wreak revenge upon an aggressor. The Royal Navy still maintains a force of conventionally equipped submarines to counter the threat of the ever-increasing Soviet nuclear submarine fleet so that, in part at least, the Silent Service remains a force capable of striking at other ships. There can be little doubt however that the most potent weapon in the entire armoury of the Royal Navy is her Polaris submarine, a devastatingly formidable deterrent to global warfare. At a cost of almost forty million pounds each, these submarine giants are perhaps Britain's surest investment for world peace.

Bibliography

In the course of his research the author has referred to the following books for background information and technical details. They are recommended to the reader who wishes to delve deeper into the subject of submarines, their history and development.

Submariners V.C., Rear-Admiral Sir William Jameson, RN (Peter Davies, 1962)

The submarine and sea power, Vice-Admiral Sir Arthur Hezlet, RN (Peter Davies, 1967)

The war at sea, Captain S. W. Roskill, RN (3 Vols) (HM Stationery Office, 1960, 1962, 1966)

Above us the waves, C. E. T. Warren and James Benson (Harrap, 1953)

U-boats under the swastika, Jak Malmann Schowell (Ian Allan, 1973)

'Subsunk': Story of submarine escape, W. O. Shelford (Harrap, 1918)

Fighting under the sea, Captain Donald Macintyre, RN (Evans Bros, 1965)

The British submarine, Commander F. W. Lipscomb, RN (Adam & Charles Black, 1954)

A damned un-English weapon, Edwyn Gray (Seeley, Service & Co, 1971)

The battle of the Atlantic, Captain Donald Macintyre, RN (Batsford, 1961)

Warships, H. T. Lenton (Hamlyn, 1970)

The K Boats, Don Everitt (Harrap, 1963)

158

The Imperial Japanese Navy, A. J. Watts and B. G. Gordon (Macdonald, 1971)

The wonderful story of the sea, edited by Harold Wheeler (Odhams Press)

Against all odds, Thomas Gallagher (Macdonald, 1971)

Dardanelles patrol, Peter Shankland and Anthony Hunter (Collins, 1964)

One of our submarines, Commander Edward Young, RNV(S)R (Hart-Davis, 1953)

Will not we fear, C. E. T. Warren and James Benson (Harrap, 1961)

Mein weg nach Scapa Flow, Günter Prien (Deutscher Verlag, 1940)

U-boat – the secret menace, David Mason (Macdonald, 1968)

German secret weapons, Brian Ford (Macdonald, 1970)

The challenge of war, Guy Hartcup (David & Charles, 1970)

Raiders of the deep, Lowell Thomas (Heinemann, 1929)

Divine thunder, Bernard Millot (Macdonald, 1971)

American submarines, H. T. Lenton (Macdonald, 1973)

German surface warships, H. T. Lenton (Macdonald, 1966)

Sink the Tirpitz, Leonce Peillard (Cape, 1968)

German submarines, H. T. Lenton (Macdonald, 1965)

Secrets and stories of the war (Readers Digest, 1963)

Profile warship No. 34 – U.S.S. Barb, Commander W. H. Cracknell, USN (Profile Publications, 1973)

Profile warship No. 16 – H.M. S/M Upholder, Captain M. L. C. Crawford, RN (Profile Publications, 1972)

The encyclopedia of military history, R. Ernest Dupuy and Trevor N. Dupuy (Macdonald, 1970)

World War 1939–45, Brigadier Peter Young (Arthur Barker, 1966)

The sea our heritage, J. G. Lockhart (Geoffrey Bles, 1940)

The battle of the seas, Sir Archibald Hurd (Hodder & Stoughton, 1941)

Roger Keyes, Cecil Aspinall-Oglander (The Hogarth Press, 1951)

Encyclopedia of ships, Enzo Angelucci (Odhams Books, 1970)

The frogmen, Tom Waldron and James Gleeson (Evans Bros, 1950)

Suicide weapon, Lt Colonel A. J. Barker (Pan/Ballantine, 1972)

History of the First World War (Series) (BPC Publishing, 1971)

History of the Second World War (Series) (Purnell & Sons, 1966)

History of the First World War, Sir Basil Liddell Hart (Cassell, 1970)

History of the Second World War, Sir Basil Liddell Hart (Cassell, 1970)

My mystery ships, Vice-Admiral Gordon Campbell (Hodder & Stoughton, 1928)

History of the Great War – the Merchant Navy (3 Vols), Sir Archibald Hurd (1921, 1924, 1929)